The
Improvement of College Worship

By

PAUL N. ELBIN, Ph.D.

Teachers College, Columbia University
Contributions to Education, No. 530

Bureau of Publications
Teachers College, Columbia University
NEW YORK CITY
1932

Copyright, 1932, by TEACHERS COLLEGE, COLUMBIA UNIVERSITY

ACKNOWLEDGMENTS

The author is deeply grateful to Professor Adelaide Teague Case, whose constant attention to this study in every stage of its preparation was his encouragement and guide. Gratitude is due Professor R. B. Raup and Professor R. B. Spence for their thoughtful criticisms and guidance throughout the study. The author wishes also to express his appreciation of the never-failing inspiration and help of his wife, Helen Pierce Elbin.

P. N. E.

CONTENTS

CHAPTER	PAGE
INTRODUCTION: *The Purpose and Nature of this Study*	1

I. *What Is the Present Situation?* 5
   A. Purposes of worship expressed by the leaders 7
   B. Evidences of success claimed by the leaders 14
   C. Student opinion toward chapel as interpreted by college administrators 17
   D. Student opinion as reflected in college newspaper editorials . 26
   E. Summary 31

II. *On What Basis May We Improve Chapel Services?* 32
   A. What are the modern basic theories of worship? . . . 32
   B. What purpose of worship is here suggested? 46
   C. What standards for guidance in the preparation and conduct of worship services for students do we need? . . 50

III. *How May We Solve Certain Practical Problems in the Administration of Chapel Services?* 59
   A. Leadership of the services 59
   B. Frequency and hour of the services 63
   C. The content of the services 65
   D. Music 68
   E. Silent worship 75

IV. *How May We Prepare Actual Services of Worship for Chapel?* . 79
   A. Explanatory 79
      1. The question of ritualism 79
      2. The order of service 82
      3. The selection of themes for the services 89
        (with suggestive calendars) 90
   B. Illustrative Services 95
      1. Services with ethical purposes 95
        a. In devotion to racial brotherhood 95
        b. For international peace 97
        c. For social justice 100
        d. In preparation for Christmas 102
        e. For Christmas 103
        f. In praise of sincerity 106

vi Contents

CHAPTER		PAGE
2. Services of appreciation		107
g. In praise of the beauties of autumn (Nature)		107
h. In appreciation of winter (Nature)		109
i. For true sportsmanship (personal problems)		112
j. For New Year's (personal problems)		113
k. In appreciation of friendship (other people)		114
l. Of dedication to Jesus the Christ (Jesus)		116
V. What Materials Can We Find for Use in Services of Worship?		119
Introductory: Bases of Compilation		119
Classified index of worship materials		124
1. Art and music		125
2. Beatitudes		125
3. Beginning of school		125
4. Chastity		126
5. Christmas		126
6. Church		127
7. Commencement; close of school		127
8. Consecration		127
9. Courage		128
10. Creeds		128
11. Deceit		128
12. Doubts		129
13. Easter		129
14. Education		129
15. Envy		130
16. Evening		130
17. Faith		130
18. Finances		130
19. Forgiveness		131
20. Freedom		131
21. Friendship		131
22. Health		132
23. Holy Week		132
24. Home; parents		132
25. Jesus, call of		133
26. Joy of life		133
27. Kingdom of God		133
28. Laborers		133
29. Martyrdom		134
30. Memorial		134
31. Morning		134
32. Nature		134

Contents vii

	PAGE
33. New Year	135
34. Patriotic	135
35. Peace (inner)	136
36. Peace (national)	136
37. Quest for God	136
38. Racial brotherhood	136
39. Repentance	137
40. Self-control	137
41. Service; love	138
42. Sportsmanship	138
43. Sunday	138
44. Thanksgiving; praise	138
45. Work	139
Bibliography of materials for use in college chapels	139

APPENDIX
A. The Questionnaire 147
B. List of Coöperating Schools 149
C. Books Listed in Replies to Questionnaires as Having Been of Value in the Preparation of Services for College Worship 151
D. Bibliography 152

The Improvement of College Worship

INTRODUCTION

THE PURPOSE AND NATURE OF THIS STUDY

The problems of college presidents, deans, chaplains, and faculty members who conduct chapel services are numerous and important. Unlike the task of the average minister, whose work in leading worship is done mainly on Sundays, the leaders of college worship must plan services from one to seven times a week. Many of these leaders, especially in state and non-sectarian schools, do not feel free to follow the practices of any one denomination. Perhaps many more do not wish to be so limited. Their congregations are unlike the average church congregations. The crowds of young people who flock to college chapels, some by compulsion, some voluntarily, present to the person delegated to lead their worship problems which are not easily solved. The difficulties inherent in the work have been made only more acute by the severe criticism which has been freely given. These criticisms, while revealing that in some colleges the chapel service is in the rut that appears to be its grave, should arouse the leaders of college worship to analyze their work and to plan to meet intelligently difficulties which all agree to be tremendous.

The questions with which this study deals are as follows:

1. What is the present situation with regard to the worship services conducted in college chapels; that is, what are the leaders trying to do, what do they think they are accomplishing, and in what way do they interpret the student attitude?
2. What objectives may college worship seek?
3. What standards for guidance in the preparation and conduct of worship services intended for students may we logically use?

4. How may we improve certain practical aspects of the administration of chapel services?
5. How may we prepare actual services of worship for college chapels?
6. What materials can we find for use in such services?

The problem of the study, then, is the improvement of college chapel services considered from the non-sectarian or the Protestant viewpoint. Underlying the study is the obvious assumption that many institutions will continue to hold such services.

The first step in the investigation was the endeavor to learn, through the questionnaire method, something of the practices, purposes, and problems of representative leaders of college worship. The questionnaire was used because it promised the most complete and accurate answers to the questions which it was desired should be answered by leaders of college chapel services. Questions of fact could easily be checked by those who knew from their own experience and questions of theory could be answered in any accurate way by no other people. Accordingly, a questionnaire was sent to the "chaplain or the person responsible for chapel or assembly" of 176 American institutions of higher learning of various types. The distribution of these inquiries to the several types of schools was determined to an approximate degree by the number and enrollment of schools according to the latest U. S. Biennial Survey of Education.[1]

The number of questionnaires sent to the various types of schools follows:

[1] *Biennial Survey of Education 1926–1928.* Department of the Interior, Bureau of Education. Bulletin 1930, No. 16. U. S. Government Printing Office, 1930. According to this report the following is the division of institutions of higher learning in this country.
  1. There are 850 private colleges, universities, and professional schools with a total enrollment of 533,789.
  2. There are 226 public colleges, universities, and professional schools with a total enrollment of 335,009.
  3. There are 248 junior colleges with a total enrollment of 44,855.
  4. There are 206 teachers colleges and normal schools with a total enrollment of 274,348.
  5. There are 176 schools of theology with a total enrollment of 13,642.

Schools of other specialized types were not considered to be of special interest in this study. The distribution of questionnaires among the types of schools listed above was based not only on the statistics given but also on the probability of the value of replies in indicating the real situation with regard to college chapels. The figures above were used to preserve a balance in the grouping of the questionnaires.

78 to private colleges and universities
38 to publicly controlled colleges and universities
25 to junior colleges
25 to teachers colleges and normal schools
10 to theological seminaries

The selection of the schools within these groups was determined largely by the desire to obtain a wide geographical and denominational variety. Of the total 176, 109 schools were privately controlled and 67 were publicly controlled. A copy of the questionnaire will be found in the Appendix.

Of the 176 questionnaires mailed, 108 were returned, as follows:

Privately controlled schools   70, or 64.21% of the number sent
Publicly controlled schools   38, or 56.71% of the number sent

Total   108, or 61.30% of the number sent

Four of the returned forms were not usable. One state-controlled school had been discontinued, and three of the questionnaires returned by private colleges were, in the main, unanswered. The questionnaires used in the summaries to be presented, therefore, represent 67 privately controlled colleges and 37 publicly controlled colleges, a total of 104.

It is interesting to note the wide geographical distribution of the colleges. Replies were received from at least one college in each of forty-four states, every state except Mississippi, New Mexico, Rhode Island, and North Dakota. Ohio contributed the largest number of replies from any one state—ten; New York and Pennsylvania rank second with seven each.[2]

[2] The exact distribution of the replies by states is as follows:

Alabama	1	Louisiana	1	Oklahoma	2
Arizona	1	Maine	2	Oregon	1
Arkansas	2	Maryland	2	Pennsylvania	7
California	4	Massachusetts	6	South Carolina	1
Colorado	1	Michigan	3	South Dakota	1
Connecticut	2	Minnesota	1	Tennessee	1
Delaware	1	Missouri	3	Texas	3
Florida	1	Montana	1	Utah	1
Georgia	1	Nebraska	1	Vermont	1
Idaho	2	Nevada	1	Virginia	6
Illinois	4	New Hampshire	1	Washington	1
Indiana	4	New Jersey	2	West Virginia	4
Iowa	1	New York	7	Wisconsin	2
Kansas	1	North Carolina	5	Wyoming	1
Kentucky	4	Ohio	10		

Equally interesting, perhaps, is the denominational distribution of the replies from the private schools. Not all denominations are represented, by any means, but there are enough to guarantee that the replies will not take on the flavor of any particular denomination. Of the 67 privately controlled institutions reporting, 20 are non-sectarian, 11 Presbyterian, 10 Methodist Episcopal, 1 Methodist Presbyterian, 8 Baptist, and 5 Lutheran.[3]

An effort was made to supplement this investigation by any other similar studies made in the past. One or two such summaries will be found here.

The futility of any attempts to set up worship objectives by scientific research was recognized. In this study an investigation of current theories of worship was made, and general tendencies were noted. A statement of possible outcomes of college worship, considered not to be inconsistent with general trends of the day nor with the purposes of college leaders of worship, was made by the author. The standards which guided the selection of materials in the latter part of the study were set forth.

Some of the practices of the colleges, as revealed in the questionnaire, were then given and some suggestions for improvement were made. The actual working out of services of worship in harmony with the theories developed during the study was attempted in Chapter IV. Then followed the search for materials to be used in such services of worship. This mass of materials might constitute a source book for leaders of college worship who find the theories of student-centered worship expressed in this book acceptable to them.

It is the sincere hope of the author that this study may inspire a general evaluation of the objectives, methods, and materials in use in many college chapels, and that it may point the way to improvement in an element of the American college which is historically important but which is frequently lagging in our educational progress.

[3] The remainder of the replies are distributed as follows:

United Brethren	2	Friends	1
Disciples	2	Holiness	1
Christian	1	Latter Day Saints	1
Christian-Congregational	1	Seventh Day Advent	1
Congregational	1	African M. E.	1
Methodist Presbyterian	1		

CHAPTER I

WHAT IS THE PRESENT SITUATION?

All the sixty-seven privately controlled schools reporting state that some kind of religious service is held under their auspices. Sixty-five hold week-day chapel services; two Sunday chapel only. Figures below apply only to the former. Of the thirty-seven state schools reporting, seventeen have some kind of religious services conducted for students by officers of the school; twenty have no such services. Administrators of state schools, classified by their attitude toward chapel services, may be divided into three groups. First, there are those who, either by law or by personal choice, hold no services and appear to be generally indifferent to the question. Two phases of this attitude are shown in these two letters of college presidents:

> No chapel exercises permitted in state schools.

> The religious work at ———— University is conducted for the most part by the representatives of the different churches in the country and by Christian associations. We do not have a regular religious chapel service.

Second, there are administrators of state schools who have no distinctly religious services in their schools at regular intervals but who are concerned about the religious life of their students. This attitude is well stated in this letter from the president of an Ohio college:

> We frequently sing gospel songs by the school, but not regularly. We occasionally use a scripture lesson but not regularly. We occasionally have a minister address the assembly but not often. The president speaks more often than any one else, and always tries to stress educational, civic, moral or religious ideals, but our assemblies are seldom distinctly religious meetings.
> On the other hand, we urge the students to take advantage of the religious services of the community; to identify themselves with some church while they are in College; and to support the voluntary

religious associations connected with the College—Y. M. C. A., Y. W. C. A., Vesper services, etc.

Personally I have been actively identified with a Protestant church all my life; an Elder in the Presbyterian church more than twenty years, and still highly appreciative of the place of the church and its importance in our present-day life. But I am inclined to think that the indirect influence of religious teachers in the ordinary classroom in college, — teachers who have been able to think their way through Psychology, Biology, and other sciences, and still keep their grip upon fundamentals in religion—is a more potent one than formal exercises of worship even in a college chapel.

And, third, there are administrators of state schools, seventeen of thirty-seven reporting, who arrange to have non-sectarian devotional services conducted for their students, usually as a preliminary part of an assembly program composed mainly of non-religious elements.

The questionnaire was sent to the "chaplain or the person responsible for chapel or assembly." In most cases the answers were prepared by those actively in charge. For the privately controlled schools the answers were given by the following:

Presidents	31
Professors	13
Deans	12
Chaplains or college pastors	10
No name given	1

For the publicly controlled schools the answers were given by the following:

Presidents	15
Secretaries	9
Professors	5
Chaplains	4
Deans	4
No name given	1

It is interesting to note that a letter addressed to "the person responsible for chapel or assembly" was answered, in most cases, by the president. The questionnaires indicate that the presidents of colleges are inclined to take considerable personal interest in the chapel service.

In this chapter the present situation in college chapels will be reviewed mainly through the eyes of these leaders. Their objectives in holding chapel services will be given, their evidences of success in attaining these objectives will be revealed, and their interpretation of student attitudes in their institutions will be shown. Finally, though the predominant viewpoint of this study is that of the faculty leader of worship, some notice will be taken of editorial opinion in student newspapers.

A. Purposes of Worship Expressed by the Leaders

The leaders of worship were asked, "What do you hope to accomplish with your worship services? (Your fundamental purposes of worship are desired. Try to avoid vague, general statements.)" Sixty schools answered the question, fifty-two private schools from sixty-seven having chapel and eight public schools from seventeen having chapel. These sixty schools gave eighty-three different purposes of worship. In the following classification the eighty-three replies are grouped under headings which express the various purposes mentioned. There is frequently some overlapping because one sentence may contain more than one purpose, but so related to one another that division seems inadvisable. Eleven different objectives were discovered among the eighty-three replies received. These objectives are stated below in inclusive form and below them the exact words of the replies are given.

1. The building of character was the purpose given by the largest number agreeing to any one answer, seventeen in all. In many of the answers character is identified with service and good will. The answers follow:

> Character building.
> To promote the idea of service.
> To lead the students to see how men should live together for the best good of all.
> To strengthen the moral fibre of the student and faculty group.
> To get students to see the highest meaning of their experiences and to dedicate themselves to this highest.
> Inspiration for service.
> Develop a sense of the reality of religion and furnish a religious dynamic for worthy character and everyday living.
> To get religion "under the skin and not on top of it." To let them realize that true religion means no profanity, no cheating, no immorality.

Translation of religion into life; Son of God into Son of Man; right faith into moral living.

To awaken in the students a consistent desire for an intelligent, constructive Christian life.

A love and reverence for worship and in the end consecration of life to service.

To bring each one under the teaching of Jesus, to the extent that he will seek to exemplify the teaching in his life.

To send out Christian women full of faith and eager to serve life.

A guidance toward the building of attitudes and ideals.

We hope to teach them the connection between worship and everyday living.

The building of more Christlike *ideals* in reference to everyday living, a broader, richer, optimistic outlook on life. A sensitivity to the needs of mankind and a passion to do something about it. In short, a realization that religion has to do with life.

2. The creation and maintenance of an interest in religion and in spiritual affairs was the purpose which ranked second in number of replies, fifteen in all subscribing to the theory that college worship is valuable if it sustains such an interest. A few of these replies express hope that other results will follow, while others are content to create attitudes of respect toward things religious. The answers are:

To keep the students interested in spiritual affairs during their student days.

The purpose is to create and maintain a religious sentiment.

To commend the religious attitude toward life.

A respectful and reverential attitude toward religion—to the end that it may be given a fair trial.

To bring Christian ideals before students: to induce them to think on religion.

Develop some (even though slight) appreciation of religion.

A clear, intelligent mind on religion: i.e., educational.

Develop a sense of the reality of religion.

To create consciousness of need of worship and to minister to it.

To create a respect for religion. . . .

To create a proper attitude toward God and things religious.

To develop and to conserve the spirit of devotion and reverence.

To magnify the concept of the Deity.

A respect and reverence for religion coupled with a rational faith and consistent attitude toward life problems.

Awakening to concepts of religious experience in keeping with modern thought. Reinforcement of religious aspiration in the individual student.

To stimulate thought about God and devotion to the will or character of God.

3. Realization of the presence of God and communion with Him are the purposes of worship given in thirteen replies, ranking third. The value of communion is the thing stressed in these replies, *fellowship* with God being considered the essential element in college worship. These answers were given in the following words:

An *awareness of God!*—an appreciation of Christ.

To develop in the student a sense of the unseen presence. To foster the idea that there is more in life than can be supplied by classroom work.

To bring to the students a recognition of spiritual values. To bring about communion with God.

To show the students that God has a place in every life every day.

A moment of daily contact with God through prayer, meditation, music. The emotional element enters here.

To direct the thought of the student to a Supreme Being on whose love and care they are dependent.

Communion with God, spiritual growth. . . .

Sense of fellowship with one another and God, reverence, meditation.

A mood of sensitiveness, appreciation of the best, sense of the Divine presence.

To create a sense of presence and communion with God.

Fellowship with God through Jesus Christ. Everything must be done to develop the consciousness of God.

To cultivate and express a sense of spiritual realities and moral values, according to Christian standards.

Fellowship in communion with God and in facing the big questions of human life.

4. Nine reported that the purpose of chapel was to provide a time and place for meditation. It will be seen throughout the summary of these replies that there is overlapping between the groupings. For instance, some of the nine may have communion with God in mind when they say meditation. Nevertheless, the answers do divide somewhat as given in the summaries here. Those who seek meditation answer:

To offer to those who attend, a quiet half-hour in the middle of the week for reflection and consideration of spiritual affairs.

Retrospection and meditation on spiritual values.
To contribute for a little while the mood of worship.
Occasion for meditation and reflection.
Reverence, meditation.
Meditation is important in the scheme of civilization. In the pursuit of higher education a reverence for God is an excellent attribute.
No information so much as inspiration, and encouragement toward an attitude of worship, and a choice of worthwhile things in life.
To drive home the need and worth of daily religious meditation and prayer.
The most that can be gained is to give the student a set time and opportunity for moral (personal) introspection.

5. Seven of the persons replying value college worship for its beneficial effect on the general life of the college rather than for its individual benefits. These are the results they expect:

We believe that a spiritual or religious attitude should dominate college life, and chapel services distinctly contribute toward it.
To give tone to the spiritual life of the campus.
To deepen the spiritual life of the assembly; and strengthen the moral fibre of the student and faculty group.
The University of ——— is a Christian college in name and this is the method we use to make it Christian in reality.
To unify the group into a community of students who desire the college to be a place of high ideals and noble struggle.
To create and maintain a religious atmosphere.
1. Corporate worship. 2. School assembly objectives. 3. Educational values.

6. Six gave rather general answers which can scarcely be classified:

Receptive and interested attitude.
To meet the religious needs of the individual student.
Definite preparation of leaders of devotional exercises.
Those things which are usually sought in any Christian service of worship.
Reality of devotion.
We seek to maintain a spirit of religious devotion.

7. Four said that chapel was for the purpose of helping with the day's work:

Attaining a proper mood to begin the day.
To enable the student and teacher to gain a calm poise and strength for the day.

To give freshness and vitality to the work of the day by the reverent worship.

Two classes precede and two follow chapel. We like to think it is a period of relaxation from class strains.

8. Four seemed to have in mind some mental hygienic values of worship, the possibility of helping students with problems of personality, career, etc.:

To supply the sense of spiritual unity in hectic lives of students.

To aid the process of integration in people. To establish a balance in the presence of intellectual and physical activities.

To help in the formulation of life purposes. . . . Help in the solution of student problems: intellectual, social, personal.

A sense of fellowship in a common adventure. A recognition of human nature's great possibilities. An understanding of life's meaning.

9. Four of the answers mentioned instruction as one of the important purposes of their chapel worship:

. . . Knowledge of Bible, familiarity with great hymns.

To impress the worth of the Bible: to encourage its study.

Religious instruction. Character building.

We hope to teach students *how* to worship.

10. Two schools—two answers out of eighty-three—state that the purpose of chapel is to win converts to Christ:

To get students to accept Christ as personal Saviour.

To elevate the Christ. . . .

11. Two answers seemed to doubt that college worship is much more than a matter of form:

I doubt if such devotionals are of much religious value. It is largely a matter of "form" and tradition. Devotional worship does not mix with "pep" meetings and many secular addresses. A worship program should be given on Sunday.

An opportunity for those who wish to attend non-sectarian religious exercises.[1]

[1] A comparison of the foregoing replies, written in the autumn of 1930, with a somewhat similar study published in 1926, is interesting. In March 1926 Dr. A. P. Kephart published in the *Educational Review* (pp. 146–52) an article entitled "The Problem of College Chapel Exercises" in which he summarized 392 replies which he received from questionnaires sent to 623 American colleges. The reasons given for requiring attendance at chapel exercises were as follows:

An analysis of these professed objectives by leaders of college worship reveals several things:

1. The obvious lack of agreement among the leaders of college worship. Not more than seventeen replies (out of eighty-three) could honestly be grouped under more than one heading. That does not mean that the holding of one of the purposes precludes holding any others, for, indeed, many of the leaders gave more than one purpose (sixty leaders gave eighty-three objectives). But it is apparent that if the primary aim of worship is communion with God, the aim of a service embodying that purpose will not be merely the creation of an attitude of respect for things religious. If character building is the essential aim of college worship, the purpose is not merely to help with the day's work. If meditation is the real purpose of college worship, conversion to Christ is not also the immediate aim.

Unity	55	Religious and moral value	12
Spiritual value	34	Keep Christian atmosphere	10
Part of college work	24	Inspiration	4
Morale	22	Loyalty	3
Announcements	19	Duty	2
Formation of habits	13	Provide audience for speaker	1
Educational value	13		
Worship	12	Miscellaneous	3

It is difficult to compare these findings with the findings of the present study because Dr. Kephart's replies deal with reasons for requiring attendance, and, besides, are very vaguely classified.

A more recent report on this subject is found in *Religion in the American College* by Edward Sterling Boyer (Abingdon Press, 1930). In his report of a survey of twenty-six typical church colleges with respect to chapel exercises, Mr. Boyer writes (p. 36): "The claims for a religious contribution of chapel were made in the following terms: cultivation of rational religious attitudes and habits; creating interest and reverence for sacred principles; giving group and institutional sanctions to religious ideals and practices; and cultivating habits of worship as a normal aspect of daily life. . . . Five of the colleges reported that they did not aim to make any religious contribution through the chapel exercises. One returned the statement that their aim was to make a religious contribution, but they failed to do so."

The report of an inquiry sponsored by the Institute of Social and Religious Research includes reasons for chapel services found in an inquiry which held more than 1100 interviews with students and faculty members in twenty-three colleges and universities. The report says:

"The chief reasons for chapel exercises given to the inquiries were not religious value, but tradition, social unification of the student body and administrative convenience."

The latter included such items as "announcements, place for visitors to speak, gets students up in mornings, a get-together."

2. The vagueness of the replies. It may be that the request for "fundamental purposes of worship" partially accounts for the vagueness of most of the replies. Perhaps the leaders in their desire to be inclusive considered their work from the general standpoint of an entire school year and not from the viewpoint of the leader of a certain service of worship. Few indicate what they include in "character building." Very few show that they attempt to meet specific needs.

3. The lack of conscious adaptation to the peculiar needs of college students. Most of the replies could be applied equally well to ordinary church worship. They probably apply to college worship to a large degree, but a considerable number fail to show any real effort to conduct services of worship intelligently based on the characteristics of their specialized congregations.

4. The emphasis on character and Christian living. It is significant that the largest group of replies emphasize these things. This shows a desire—somewhat vague, it is true—to make the chapel service effective in actual life.

5. The large number of replies giving a development of interest in religion as an objective. In this respect the objectives differ from those of the average church, whose congregation is already "interested" in religion. And in this respect the replies indicate a consciously planned program of worship based on student thought.

6. The comparatively small place for the mystical element in worship is significant. Although that group of replies ranks third, the replies total only thirteen out of eighty-three, for no other group may properly be termed mystical.

7. The very small number of replies using terms which indicate any deliberate use of the growing interest in worship as a means of mental hygiene is also significant. What values of this sort college worship has are largely derivative and not primary.

8. The very small number of replies giving instructional aims is likewise valuable in analyzing college worship. Unless we include the development of an interest in religion as instruction, which is not done here, instruction—in Bible, hymnology, worship, etc.— is a very minor element in college worship.

9. The almost total absence of the evangelistic aim is particularly interesting.

B. Evidences of Success Claimed by the Leaders

We have seen in the preceding section what worship leaders in colleges are trying to do with their services. The question in the questionnaire which immediately followed the request for this statement of objectives was this: What evidence of success [in achieving this purpose of worship] have you? The "success," of course, has to do with the influence of the chapel on the students and with their attitude toward chapel. Not all the replies included an answer to this question, but enough did to make this question one of the most valuable of all. A natural tendency to exaggerate the evidence might have been expected, but the fact that the largest group of replies was the group giving little or no evidence of success indicates considerable frankness. Forty-eight cited evidence of success of some kind as listed below; thirteen admitted that they had little or no evidence. It is possible that the latter group may mean that the effect of chapel services cannot be measured. It may be said with all fairness that few of the leaders gave proof of having any evidence of success which would be very encouraging to them. It is true that the objectives of the leaders determine their answers to this question, but the personal testimony of a few students and graduates is hardly conclusive evidence of success for most of the theories previously given.

Classified answers to the question are quoted below:

What Evidence of Success in Achieving the Purpose of Your Worship Have You?

1. Thirteen said they had little or no evidence of success:

    Not much, I regret to say.
    Not much. Average attendance last year about 200 out of 2000 students.
    Moderate. I refrain from expressing opinion.
    None.
    Little, except there is a small group who testify.
    No tangible evidence.
    Little. We think there is at least a more sympathetic attitude toward chapel.
    Through a critical period services held their own and are strongly commended as well as criticized. The issue is reasonably alive.
    Hard to measure, but we have a greatly improved atmosphere and a higher type of students.

Present Situation 15

We make no great claims of success. Many profess to have been helped.
The results are strictly personal. Some students get great benefit, others very little. These results cannot be noted down because they are unknown.
Only occasional.
We do not expect to see much evidence as chapel is given to directions and announcements.

2. Ten cited good attendance as evidence of their success:

An increased attendance. . . .
A satisfactory attendance. . . .
Small but fairly regular attendance for the 3½ years we have been having this form of chapel.
Large and appreciative attendance, although no check on attendance is made.
The assemblies are attended by most of the students even though attendance is optional.
A required chapel to which there is practically no objection on the part of 1600 students.
Large voluntary service.
Voluntary service attended by about 80% of students.
Through a critical period services held their own. . . .
A fine response from both student and faculty group, good attendance.

3. Ten cited good attention at chapel as evidence of success:

The average attitude during service is excellent.
Attention and response from students.
Students' attitude during service has improved greatly.
Good attendance, reverence, participation.
Students are respectful towards things religious.
Good attention and active participation by most students.
A satisfactory attendance and a satisfactory behaviour of those who attend.
Students follow the service attentively.
Reverent attention.
Respectful attitude at least.

4. Nine gave favorable testimony of students as their evidence:

A number of the students have expressed high appreciation for the Wednesday chapel service.
Many purely voluntary statements of the students.
Personal testimonies of students. . . .

Much expressed appreciation of service on part of students.
Individual reaction within the student body.
Individual students tell me of their appreciation of chapel.
Many expressions on the part of students past and present that they have found our chapel period not a bore but a helpful experience.
Many students have told me that they have been greatly benefited.
Many profess to have been helped.

5. Six cited as evidence of success the fact that most of their students accepted Christ, joined the church, or went out in service:

Practically all of our girls come before the end of the year to definite decision about Christ.
Most students become Christians.
The large number of alumnae who engage in service after graduation.
Out of more than 700 graduates only 2 have failed to identify themselves with some church before graduation.
Our student body is almost 100% Christian. They go out in Christian service as ministers, missionaries, Christian laymen.
A third of our students can be called on to lead chapel at any time.

6. Four cited the testimony of graduates as evidence of success:

The testimony of returning students.
Expression of appreciation later on by alumni.
Almost universal report from graduates of the institution that chapel was most helpful factor during their four years here.
Many expressions on the part of students past and present that they have found our chapel period not a bore but a helpful experience.

7. Four cited improved college spirit and morality as evidence:

The spirit of the school is a testimony.
College unification has never been better. Fine spirit of unity in college.
The character of our student body, as testified to by guest speakers.
We have a greatly improved atmosphere and a higher type of student. Fewer campus sins.

8. Four cited interest in services as evidence of success:

Greater interest on the part of both student and faculty leaders.
In seven years our services have been worshipful, orderly, and though required have the support of student opinion. Vespers the students love.

Interest, attention, and response from students.
Continued interest in the services.

C. STUDENT OPINION TOWARD CHAPEL AS INTERPRETED BY COLLEGE ADMINISTRATORS

Following are classified answers to the questions: 1. How would you describe in a few words the prevailing student attitude toward chapel in your institution? 2. To what extent do you estimate that there is a student sentiment for radical change either in attendance rules or in the conduct of the services?

I. PRIVATE SCHOOLS (59 REPLIES OUT OF 67 QUESTIONNAIRES)

A. PRIVATE SCHOOLS WHERE ATTENDANCE IS REQUIRED (46 SCHOOLS)

1. General Student Attitude

1. Twenty-six reported that student sentiment was generally favorable:

On the whole, amiable.
It is a source of inspiration and pleasure.
On a recent poll only 80 out of 1300 voting suggested lifting requirement. One of scale of 1–7, 550 rated it one, 1050 three or better as to religious helpfulness.
Very good. Taken as part of program. If administration and faculty assume it high importance, students will.
A few make sporadic objection to requirement, but the student body as a whole seem to appreciate.
Part of their regular program. Appreciated by the students as very interesting and educational in character.
Expressions from students have been called for from time to time, orally and in writing. No large demand for change.
As nearly that of children toward the well-regulated family altar as can be described.
All seem to admire vespers—bring their folks. We have a chorus of eighty. Chapel is taken for granted. When we ask student council whether chapel should be voluntary the usual reply is, "Why open the question?"
They mostly like it and when they don't attend it is due to indolence or because they have no campus engagements at 9.
Friendly.
Generally good. Only a few object. Most of them are enthusiastic.
Very sympathetic, since we have an unusually attractive band or

orchestra and give students ample time, after the devotional, as their own as a clearing house of all student activities.

In general, students are very coöperative.

Last year I held a number of discussion groups with students on how we could improve chapel. Put them on chapel committee. Had each class lead chapel for a week each. Their response and attitude has been and is fine.

Reverent and interested.

A great majority of our students appreciate chapel and enjoy it. A few, of course, think it is a bore and irksome. That is to be expected.

Respectful and appreciative.

Their attitude is splendid.

Worshipful generally, respectful always.

The inspirational period of the day's work.

Accepted as an important part of the school program.

Friendly for the most part.

Appreciative.

Friendly for the most part.

No sentiment for change.

2. Eight reported that their students were merely indifferent to chapel:

Uninterested.

Submissive or acquiescent rather than antagonistic or enthusiastic.

One of willingness, though the attendance would be small without compulsion.

Acceptance, toleration, reconciliation describe somewhat the *group* attitude. A great number of individuals present are very sympathetic.

The majority are passive or agreeable.

Students take it as a matter of course.

Probably that it [chapel] is improving. A few years ago chapel was chaotic and quite unpopular. We have tried to make it more dignified. No compulsory service is popular, but it is more respected.

Unconcern and patronizing tolerance.

3. Eight reported that their student bodies were divided in their attitude toward chapel:

Some objection to the compulsory element, but no antagonism evident.

There is no "prevailing" attitude. There is favorable comment, unfavorable, and much indifference.

The majority of the students like the order of worship and especially the use we make of music in it, but they are critical of the average devotional talk.
None are antagonistic, some are indifferent, the majority enjoy it.
After a semester's experimentation I think the students are won over to a compulsory assembly. They have voted to do so through their student council. But a compulsory *chapel* they would not want.
A few students clamor for voluntary chapel once in a while. When the speaker is good, interest is alert and reverent. Poor speakers invite inattention in chapel as everywhere else.
No prevailing attitude. Many have kindly and interested attitude; many are bored, or at least indifferent; none actively oppose or ridicule.
Some would like to abolish it, but if it came to a real issue my impression is that the student body would vote overwhelmingly to keep it.

4. Two report that their students are generally unfavorable to chapel:

The *general* attitude, I believe, is that chapel is a nuisance, to be joked about in the college paper, but which they would really hate to see abolished.
A youth tendency. "We know what we want." "We see no need of it." Students have not found themselves.

2. *Degree of Sentiment for Change in Required Chapel Situations*

1. Twenty-six reported that there is very little or no sentiment against either the conduct of chapel or the attendance rules:

None for radical change.
No sentiment for change in conduct of worship and very little sentiment for doing away with compulsory chapel.
We have never had any serious criticism or protest on the part of the students against chapel attendance.
No more than on my part, to find a more helpful type of service.
Nothing marked.
The required chapel is accepted here and it is not a question in the minds of the students. A few years ago there was some discussion but at present none.
None so far as I know. Student insurgence is not centering at that point just now, though it may do so at any time. It is a divine right to criticize something.
Am aware of no such student sentiment.

I have been able to sense none.

In seven years there have been only two instances when the student paper contained letters opposing chapel. We exercise no censorship either; sometimes I wish we did.

So far as I know there is no disposition to make any changes in the services. Chapel committee composed of three faculty members and three students.

Little well-founded desire for such change. There is no intention here to abandon such exercises.

We have had no call for a change during the many years of service.

There is no apparent desire for a change here.

Almost no sentiment for change.

Have observed none.

Other answers: "None."

2. Ten reported that there is some sentiment for change, but that it is not by any means preponderant:

A number of the students individually would like a change away from required attendance, but there is no united sentiment on this point.

Not to any great extent.

A few students clamor for voluntary chapel once in a while, but we feel that the great majority are happy with the present situation.

Programs planned by a committee of students and faculty and adapted to student needs and opinions. This has somewhat changed student opposition. Many students attended last semester through sense of duty rather than through enthusiastic support.

Not over 25%.

There is some objection to the compulsory element, but no antagonism evident.

Some want a change but hard to give figures.

No large demand for change.

Many have kindly and interested attitude; many are bored or at least indifferent; none actively oppose or ridicule.

A ballot taken last week indicates no desired change. A negligible number suggested rescinding the compulsory feature.

3. Eight reported that their student sentiment was largely for radical change:

Most of the thoughtful students feel the need of several radical changes in one or both directions.

75% at least would change it.

Quite naturally the majority would like to avoid *required* attendance.

Present Situation 21

A very strong sentiment for change in compulsory attendance rule.

The general attitude is that chapel is a nuisance. . . .

Quite a large student sentiment for change. But I think it is largely the attitude that they prefer not to be bothered, especially at 7:45 a.m. Who wouldn't? No student is looking for the extra trouble and requirement.

There is a natural aversion to things religious. . . .

If chapel can be made more responsive to modern student needs, no sentiment against attendance.

B. PRIVATE SCHOOLS WHERE ATTENDANCE IS VOLUNTARY (15 SCHOOLS)

1. General Student Attitude

1. Six reported that chapel is generally appreciated:

Enjoyed by students.
It is decidedly popular.
A deep interest in it.
Sympathetic.
A favorable student response is noticeable.
Students attend regularly without compulsion.

2. Five reported that the students generally were indifferent to chapel:

Indifference or skepticism.
Indifference but no antagonism.
Tolerant.
Apathy.
Our students have come to feel that chapel attendance is out of date. They have as a rule no antipathy to chapel, but they want to be up-to-date.

3. Two remarked that chapel was enjoyed by those who attend and met apathy but no opposition from those who do not attend:

Those who come obviously like it; those who stay away seem to have no objection to its being held.
Very slight opposition; much indifference; considerable genuine interest.

4. Two failed to answer.

2. *Student Attitude with Regard to Radical Changes*

1. Little or no sentiment for changes—11 schools out of 15.
2. Sentiment for better building, 1; for better speakers, 1; for better services, 1:

   Student sentiment is for a better chapel service in a room that will seat the student body and a dignity that can't well be had in a small classroom used for chapel.
   They come more freely when they know good speakers will appear.
   A university continually demands increasingly real services.

3. One did not answer.

II. PUBLICLY CONTROLLED SCHOOLS—15 REPORTING (10 WITH REQUIRED ATTENDANCE; 5 VOLUNTARY)

1. *General Student Attitude Toward Chapel*

1. A total of five said their students were generally indifferent to chapel:

   Required:
   Students do not object to it.
   Fair.
   Voluntary:
   Indifference.
   Largely one of indifference.
   It has been regarded rather lightly. The spirit has not been hostile, however.

2. A total of five said their students were divided in their attitude:

   Required:
   From casual acceptance to willing participation.
   Sometimes apathetic, frequently quite valuable.
   Assemblies bore some. Others enjoy going.
   Voluntary:
   Some like it; others do not.
   Students who are religiously inclined enjoy the services; others stay away.

3. Four reported a generally favorable attitude:

   Required:
   Excellent.
   Friendly.

Favorable.
Wholesome, willing to attend.

4. One reports that its students are generally unfavorable. There is a natural aversion to things religious, to speakers preaching at them rather than offering a thought for practical reasoning.

2. *Student Sentiment for Radical Changes in Chapel*

1. Total of nine reported little or no student sentiment for change:

Required:
  1. No fault found with the one class assembly one day each week.
  2. Small extent.
  3. Very little.
  4. Perhaps 10%, a guess.

Voluntary:
  1. Small extent since no one is required to attend.
  2. Many of them perhaps would just as soon see chapel abandoned, but since they are not required to attend, they say nothing about it.
  3. We have heard no complaint.
  4. Attitude is better than it was a few years ago. Most students are indifferent about convocation. Students not wholly to blame. Difficult to get speakers with real message.
  5. The students seem very much pleased with the new arrangements.

2. Five gave no answer or said they did not know:

No data.
Don't know.
No evidence.

3. One said, "There is a natural aversion to things religious."

In order to show the student attitude toward chapel in the light of the voluntary-compulsory situation, the facts in this connection revealed by the study will be given at this point.[2] The following

---

[2] The pros and cons of compulsory chapel, irrelevant to this study, are well stated by Laird T. Hites in *The Effective Christian College*, pp. 223–26. Macmillan Co., 1929. The values of college chapel are summarized by Henry W. Tweedy in "The Problem of the College Chapel" in *Religious Education* for February 1927.

information is a summary of the information concerning attendance at college chapels received through the questionnaire.

It will be noted that compulsory chapel is the rule in the private colleges reporting and that two-thirds of the publicly controlled institutions require attendance at their assemblies. Most of the administrators reporting estimate average attendances ranging from 25 per cent to 75 per cent where attendance is voluntary.

Data Concerning Attendance at College Chapels

I. Private schools:

Total answering: 64	
Required chapel	46
Voluntary chapel	17
Choice of chapel or class in ethics or Bible	1
	64

Percentage of students in attendance:

90–100% in the 46 schools where attendance is required.

> Note.—In one school Freshmen are required to attend twice a week, others only once. In another school Freshmen and Sophomores are required to attend, while the Juniors and Seniors are not required to do so. In a third school, all are required to attend except seniors.

In the eighteen schools where attendance is voluntary:

Approx. Percentage of Attendance	No. of Schools
2	2
8	2
25	4
50	4
75	5
98	1
	18

The following information about faculty attendance in twenty-four schools where faculty members are not required to attend:

Approx. Percentage of Attendance	No. of Schools
10 or less	6
25	4
50	10
75	2
90	2
	24

II. State schools:

Total answering: 15
Required chapel or assembly: 10 (Freshmen-Sophomores only in 1)
Voluntary chapel or assembly: 5
———
15

Percentage of students in attendance:

Practically all in the 10 required assemblies (noting the one exception about Freshmen-Sophomores)
Percentage attending the five voluntary assemblies:
    About 10%   in   1 school
    20–40%   in   2 schools
    40–50%   in   2 schools
Attendance of faculty where voluntary and listed in replies:
    None attend   in   1 school
    About 25% attend in   2 schools
    Nearly all attend   in   2 schools

Summary of Replies Concerning Student Attitudes

I. The general attitude:

	Private Schools			Public Schools			
	Required	Voluntary	Total	Required	Voluntary	Total	Grand Total
1. Mainly favorable	26	6	32	4	0	4	36
2. Mainly indifferent	8	5	13	2	3	5	18
3. Divided	8	2	10	3	2	5	15
4. Mainly unfavorable	2	0	2	1	0	1	3
No answer	0	2	2	0	0	0	2
			59			15	74

II. Attitude toward changes:

	Private Schools			Public Schools			
	Required	Voluntary	Total	Required	Voluntary	Total	Grand Total
1. Little or no sentiment for	26	11	37	4	5	9	46
2. Moderate degree of sentiment	10	3	13	0	0	0	13
3. Sentiment mainly for change	8	0	8	1	0	1	9
4. No answer or "don't know"	0	1	1	5	0	5	6
			59			15	74

It is natural to wonder how far one may trust the replies of the leaders concerning the attitudes shown by the students. It is not at all a question of honesty; it is largely a question of possibility. Just how accurately can the average president, dean, chaplain, or similar college officer, measure the attitude of the students toward chapel? A vote might tell, but few have been taken. A general strike against chapel might tell, but such sensational protests have not been made. The leaders must guess on the basis of the best reports they have. These bases were given in the preceding section of this chapter.

As these figures stand, however, they show that when attendance is required students are generally favorable, but when attendance is voluntary indifference is evident. Such a fact, if true, might be explained in several ways; but the reporting of this fact may have another explanation. May it not be that when students are required to attend, their indifference, not amounting to antagonism, is mistaken for a favorable attitude? They attend and say nothing. Leaders interpret this acquiescence as approval. When students are not required to attend, their indifference to chapel services is no longer in doubt. This is a possible explanation. Then, again, it is possible that many students give little or no thought to chapel. When they do have a choice, they find something else to do.

D. STUDENT OPINION AS REFLECTED IN COLLEGE NEWSPAPER EDITORIALS

For the purpose of learning what attention is paid in the editorial columns of leading student-published college papers to questions of religion and of college chapel, the files of twenty-one such publications covering the period between the opening of the fall term in 1930 to the middle of March 1931 were studied. In some cases the files were not entirely complete; where they were greatly incomplete mention of the fact will be made. Most of the files examined contained from forty to seventy issues of each paper. The papers had to be chosen on the basis of their accessibility, unfortunately, and most of the papers represent large universities with daily editions of their papers. The schools represented in this phase of the study are not altogether comparable with the schools used in the questionnaire. These schools tend to be larger than the average school included in the questionnaire, though replies from a third of these schools are included in this study. Probably the place of the chapel is less important in the life of the ordinary student in these institutions than in many denominational colleges, and it may be that the general attitude toward religion is different in some respects. With these limitations and cautions in mind, let us examine the findings. The following is a complete list of the college newspapers studied. The number following each name is the number of editorials (and published letters to the editor) which deal with chapel or religion. When a paper is starred, that paper has published one or more editorials calling the attention of the students to some important or interesting chapel speaker scheduled to appear soon:

Brown Daily Herald	0	The Amherst Student	0
*California Daily Bruin	0	*The Cornell Daily Sun	1
Columbia Spectator	1	The Daily Princetonian	1
Harvard Crimson	0	The Dartmouth	2
Indiana Daily Student	0†	The Daily Cardinal	0
New York University Daily News	0	The Minnesota Daily	0
		The Pennsylvanian	0
Ohio State Lantern	0	The Stanford Daily	0
Oregon State Barometer	0	The Wesleyan Argus	0
Penn State Collegian	0	University Daily Kansan	0†
*Syracuse Daily Orange	2	*Yale Daily News	5

† File incomplete.

The editors of these great student newspapers, about evenly divided between state and private universities, do not seem to feel any need for saying much about religion, or about the college chapel in institutions where there is a chapel. While it would not be safe to generalize too much about the interests and attitudes of the students in these schools, it does seem reasonable to assume that if there were considerable interest in the program of the college chapel or in religion in general, such interest would be more or less reflected in the content of the editorial section of the student newspaper. The very silence of such sections speaks clearly.

"It goes without saying that the function of the college to-day is not primarily religious. Religion must take its place alongside the other aspects and interests of men and women for such attention as is due it."[3] So says Dean Hawkes of Columbia Col-

[3] Hawkes, Herbert E., *College—What's the Use?* pp. 90, 91. Doubleday, Doran & Co., 1927.

lege in a statement which sounds as though it might have come from one of the editorials indicated in the list above. The following quotations from leading student papers, which are typical of the general viewpoint, will help to confirm the feeling one gets of general student indifference to religion:

From an editorial in the *Yale Daily News*, October 1, 1930:

> Soon Yale will induct into service a new University pastor, and he will find himself confronted with the problem of religious apathy on our campus. By this we do not mean that Yale stands unique as the home of the atheist and agnostic, but simply that there are comparatively few of her students who look upon religious worship and belief as a vital force in their lives. . . .

From *The Daily Illini* quoted in *The Daily Cardinal*, November 16, 1930.

> Religion is a tabooed word in bull sessions. Mention the word and students shy from the discussion. The main trouble is that college men and women, tired of attempting to believe something that they couldn't, have thrown over-board religion and are afraid to get near it again.

From the *Purdue Exponent* quoted in *The Indiana Daily Student*, October 7, 1930.

> The God of the college student—Who is it? or perhaps what is it? . . . Taking the group as a whole, it seems that there is very little thought given to the spiritual side of one's life. . . . The perplexing angle to the question of the college student's God is that there seems to be none. . . .

A slightly different attitude is taken in this editorial from a paper representing a university which recently erected a chapel building at a cost of two million dollars. A chapel service about fifteen minutes in length is held four mornings a week, during which time there are no classes.

> If an undergraduate by chance had wandered into the Chapel yesterday morning at the Morning Chapel period, he would have found emptiness. Under the arrangement in force for two years now, Morning Chapel is held four days a week only—"as if God is heard only on certain days of the week"—as a Faculty member put it. Furthermore, on these four days less than one in a hundred students attends the service. For the other 99, the period is a time to eat breakfast, read one's paper, or loaf.

The Morning Chapel period as now held, however, is more than a harmless institution. It constitutes a serious loss of time. . . .

Since the usefulness of the Morning Chapel period is not commensurate with the handicap it inflicts on the curriculum, we recommend that it be discarded. . . .[4]

The building of beautiful edifices for chapel services is the ambition of many college authorities. Indeed, greater attention is being given to that phase of college architecture than ever before in America. In the light of that fact this editorial from *The Dartmouth* of January 8, 1931 is exceedingly interesting:

. . . the primary delusion and fallacy under which religionists of the present day are laboring: that the religious spirit can by the artificial spirit of monkey-glanding be rejuvenated within the colleges and universities of the country. The delusion is not a new one. Men have for generations sought to bolster up shaky causes by spectacular methods and nothing is more spectacular or more inspiring than the rising walls and buttresses of a fine church or cathedral. That is, it is inspiring if the inspiration precedes the building. If the building be built to inspire a religious fervor which does not exist there can be nothing more certain than the failure of its purpose. . . .

. . . But more than this and aside from the question of college chapels: Shall we assume that the college and the college man must have religion to successfully survive? Shall we write it down as imperative that he must be given the religious outlook? . . . These are questions worth pondering.

Three editorials which may be termed generally friendly to the purposes of college chapel were discovered:

From an editorial in the *Yale Daily News*, October 21, 1930.

Undergraduate sentiment as voiced in communications to the NEWS, as well as editorials in these columns, has consistently deplored "the silence which hangs like a pall over Battell Chapel," and the fact that religion is but a "still, small voice" in the hubbub of campus activities.

From an editorial in the *Yale Daily News* of October 29, 1930.

"If anyone is troubled with a mind," said Professor Angell last Wednesday night, "he will be interested in that phase of human experience which we term religion." . . . Any man who is unpreju-

---

[4] Quoted from *The Daily Princetonian* by the *Yale Daily News* of October 15, 1930.

diced in his outlook upon life, as the scientific observer must be, will feel bound to examine religion. We feel that there has been far too little opportunity to effect this examination without endorsing religion at the same time. . . .

From an editorial in the *Syracuse Daily Orange*, November 19, 1930.

Syracusans are fortunate in that the daily chapel services, as well as the Sunday programs, offer them a far greater chance to attain a calm ordered purpose of life than is found in many institutions. For the very virtue of chapel attendance will do much for a poised mind.

The opinion of a college Junior is found in *Religious Education* for October 1925. He says: "To the average college student, chapel is only one more thing that he has to attend. The average student is indifferent to it; he neither likes it nor dislikes it."

In 1929 the *New Republic* published under the title *The Students Speak Out!* the best essays written by students from twenty-two colleges on the subject "College as It Might Be." Only one student mentions a chapel in his "college as it might be" and he makes it compulsory once a week. Many refer to the conservatism of the majority of the students. One says:

Besides these rare more serious students and the great mass of the mentally sterile, there is a group of half-way students, half-way in that they have revolted superficially from the Victorian mode of behaviour, but have not found an effective standard of values to replace it. . . . So after the novelty has worn off this rather vague revolt, they settle down, accept prevailing standards, go back to "Mother Church," and grow fat, bald and forty.[5]

A Canadian Press dispatch from Toronto, dated February 27, 1931, quotes A. E. F. Allen, editor of the University of Toronto *Varsity* as saying that his editorial on religion which aroused opposition in the Ontario Legislature was based "upon acquaintance with numerous students and participation in discussions. These students were entirely negative as far as religion and God were concerned," he stated.

The data with regard to student attitudes toward chapel which have been assembled here tend to confirm the opinions of the college administrators that there is considerable student indifference

[5] Lindblom, Ross C.; pp. 42, 43.

about the chapel and its worship. The extent of this indifference can not be measured accurately with the information at hand.

E. Summary

The findings presented in this chapter indicate some specific ways in which conditions in the American college chapel are not ideal. The objectives of the leaders are not always clear and there is considerable disagreement as to what they should be. The leaders have great difficulty in presenting conclusive evidence of any appreciable success in their work. They appear skeptical about the results of their work. However, most of the leaders feel that the students in their institutions are not antagonistic toward chapel. In many schools the leaders feel the students as a whole to be friendly to their aims, and in many other schools the leaders feel the students to be indifferent to their chapel program. If the editorials of twenty-one college and university newspapers are any indication of student opinion, the latter attitude is widespread.

It is not hard to find references to confirm the conclusion that the American college chapel is in need of improvement. A few years ago a writer had this to say of some thirty college chapels which he visited: "Ordinarily the service is a brief and perfunctory affair, according to my observation, dull and uninspiring beyond words. I have seldom seen any reason why it should interest even the person conducting it."[6] Dean Herbert E. Hawkes of Columbia College in his book *College—What's the Use?* says that daily chapel "in most colleges is very far from a devotional exercise."[7] In a day when every item of the college organization is being scrutinized with a view to its usefulness, the chapel service can not hide behind the skirts of sanctity and tradition any inadequacies it may have. If the historic tradition of college chapel is to be continued, it will be because the chapel has not lagged behind the classroom and the laboratory in its devotion to truth and to the needs of a new generation.

[6] Gavit, John Palmer, *College*, p. 250. Harcourt, Brace and Co., 1925.
[7] P. 95. Doubleday, Doran & Co., 1927.

CHAPTER II

ON WHAT BASIS MAY WE IMPROVE CHAPEL SERVICES?

A. What Are the Modern Basic Theories of Worship?

The improvement of college worship should proceed on the basis of the most acceptable thought on the subject. This does not mean that leaders in actual college situations will turn to experts for ready-made theories and methods, for worship is fundamentally an art, many sided and with innumerable modes of expression. It means, rather, that leaders should realize their spiritual kinship with certain groups of thinkers and worshipers and should obtain the maximum benefits from that relationship.

In order that we may find ourselves among the modern schools of thought regarding worship, we turn now to an examination of the literature representing these viewpoints. No attempt has been made to cover all the literature on the subject, but merely to include in the survey such works as will insure a complete and clear, though brief, interpretation of representative positions on worship which are likely to interest the leaders of American college chapel services conducted in the Protestant tradition. The particular references were chosen because of popular recognition of their being representative of certain viewpoints and through the recommendation of experts in the field.

One does not go very far into this literature before he discovers that to-day worship is being considered from two main positions. The first of these two positions is, perhaps, the older of the two. This is the attitude that worship is essentially a relation between man and God. The second position may not deny that this relationship is a part of worship, but it tends to emphasize the adjustment of the individual to personal wants and social demands. It may be very readily seen that the line of demarcation between these two viewpoints is not very stable. The extremes of the two positions are, of course, very far apart. But between the extremes it is often only a matter of emphasis to determine which position a given writer represents. Dr. Pratt observed such a distinction and wrote of ". . . two types of worship, one of which aims at making some kind of effect upon the Deity or in some way communicating with him, while the other seeks only to induce some desired mood or belief or attitude in the mind of the worshiper."[1] He referred to these two types as "objective" and "subjective." Pratt's general division is quoted with approval by G. J. Jordan in *A Short Psychology of Religion* and by H. W. Dresser in his *Psychology of Religion*. A study of modern worship literature will bear out some such fundamental division in modern theories of worship, as the following discussion should show.

"*Objective*" *Theories of Worship*

Dean Sperry defines worship as "the adoration of God, the ascribing of supreme worth to God, and the manifestation of reverence in the presence of God."[2] On another page he asserts:

> A service of worship may include—in the case of most Protestant churches it habitually does include—a sermon. It may contemplate the dedication of the self to the service of the neighbor as being the actual and concrete expression of devotion to God; it may define in detail the forms which that service should assume: and it may enlist its members for the prosecution of particular causes. But all these are corollaries of the act of worship and not its original interest and intention.[3]

Ross speaks of "Worship, the communion of the finite man with the eternal and infinite God. . . ."[4] Dean Weigle in the worship manual which he and Dr. Tweedy prepared defines worship as follows:

> It [worship] is a personal approach to God. . . . It seeks to communicate to Him our attitudes, to establish intercourse with Him, to enter into as direct fellowship with Him as we can. The heart of worship is prayer.[5]

---

[1] Pratt, James Bissett, *The Religious Consciousness*, p. 290. Macmillan Co., 1920.
[2] Sperry, Willard, *Reality in Worship*, p. 164. Macmillan Co., 1926.
[3] *Ibid.*, pp. 163–64.
[4] Ross, G. A. J., *Christian Worship and Its Future*, p. 18. Abingdon Press, 1927.
[5] Weigle, Luther Allen and Tweedy, Henry Hallam, *Training the Devotional Life*, pp. 6, 7. Pilgrim Press, 1919.

The concept of worship presented by Rudolf Otto, Professor of Theology in the University of Marburg, has been widely discussed. Rufus Jones condenses this concept as follows: "Rudolf Otto, in his *Das Heilige*, is, I am convinced, much closer to the truth of things when he treats the essential aspect of religion as a hushed, trembling, palpitant response of the human soul in the presence of august, majestic, mysterious, awe-inspiring realities, which produce a consciousness of what he calls the 'numinous.' His word is from the Latin *numen*, and stands for anything that transcends the finite, the known, the naturalistic, and the describable, and which moves us with awe." [6] And Professor Otto himself says, "If a man does not *feel* what the numinous is, when he reads the sixth chapter of Isaiah, then 'no preaching, singing, telling,' in Luther's phrase, can avail him." [7]

Mysticism certainly is inherent in this type of worship. "Mysticism is not a synonym for the 'mysterious.' . . . It only means that the soul of man has dealings with realities of a different order from that with which the senses deal," says Rufus Jones.[8] He continues to define mysticism by saying, "I am here concerned for the moment with mystical religion which I here define as an overbrimming experience of contact, fellowship, or even union with a larger Life which impinges on our own life." Evelyn Underhill, mystic of another type, defines worship as follows: "Worship is the little human spirit's humble adoring acknowledgment of the measureless glory of God, the only Reality—the Perfect, the Unchanging, the entirely Free." [9]

To do justice to the "objective" type of worship, we must not fail to note another aspect which it incorporates in practice. That is the relation which is made between the nature of the God worshiped and the moral and ethical life of the worshipers. Dr. Sclater presents this idea well when he says:

> The object of this great act [public worship] is, of course, God Himself; but the worshipper is man—whose sole endeavor, at such a moment, should be to present himself as he really is, before his Maker. Consequently, times of worship are occasions when man is brought

---

[6] Jones, Rufus, *New Studies in Mystical Religion*, pp. 31, 32. Macmillan Co., 1927.
[7] Otto, Rudolf, *The Idea of the Holy*, p. 63. Oxford University Press, 1925.
[8] Jones, Rufus, *op. cit.*, p. 25.
[9] Underhill, Evelyn, *Worship*, p. 3. A. R. Mowbray and Co., London.

face to face with himself, and reminded of the large, pathetic facts of his own life.[10]

William Adams Brown also expresses this idea of worship when he says:

> For what is worship? In its simplest and most fundamental meaning it is the practice of the presence of God. . . .
>
> What does it mean to practice the presence of God? It means by deliberate and intelligent effort to make explicit to consciousness the supreme fact of religion, namely, the reality and the nearness of God, to the end that God may be able to do for us, in us, and through us, and so for the world at large, what He desires.[11]

And Professor Hocking sets forth this side of worship:

> . . . Worship may be regarded as an attempt to detach oneself from everything else in uniting with God.[12]
>
> . . . Worship is false unless it is sanctioned in turn by the life that follows it. This sanction is twofold. First that it does not undermine, but rather supports, the world of other aims. The mystic must return not less a lover of men, but rather a lover in a more intense and human fashion, because it is only the true worshipper who can find the world genuinely lovable. . . .
>
> The second sanction of worship is, that the worshipper does not merely sustain, but creates. . . . The edge of the tool of will is restored, and it is eager for world-making. The man is able to fight, to oppose and suffer; he is endowed with grit, with faith. This is the moral result of true worship.[13]

Three statements, chosen to represent divergent theories of worship, must be presented before this outline of "objective" worship is satisfactory. The first is a brief statement outlining the Friends' theory of worship:

> . . . For if the Friends have any spiritual inheritance which is of significance to other seeking Christians today, it is precisely their conception of how God may be worshipped in spirit and in truth with the least possible intrusion of the human agent or of other distracting elements. . . .

---

[10] Sclater, J. R. P., *Public Worship of God*, p. 18. George H. Doran Co., 1927.
[11] Brown, William Adams, *Worship*, pp. 3, 4. Association Press, 1917.
[12] Hocking, William Ernest, *The Meaning of God in Human Experience*, p. 365. Yale University Press, 1912.
[13] *Ibid.*, pp. 439, 440.

> There is nothing to distract the eye or ear: no decorations, no music, no collection. . . . From a living silence, from a fertile meditation, then, there grows this spiritual communion. . . . The attitude, common and natural in many church services, of being led by an individual trained and appointed to promote worship is the very opposite of the ideal attitude in a Friends meeting. . . . They know that these arts [music, etc.] are the handmaids of true worship in the case of most other communions. But for themselves they have desired throughout their history to allow no human agency or prepared program to come between them and the word of God, should it be vouchsafed to his waiting people.[14]

To show how far apart in their methods mystics may be, it seems pertinent to introduce here this assertion of Evelyn Underhill in which she discusses the Friends' theory of worship:

> Further, because men are creatures of sense as well as spirit, of body as well as soul, we must bring our senses and our bodies in, and let them play their part in the worshipping act. Thus Quaker silence, in itself most precious, is not really enough for full Christian worship. It is based on a virtual antithesis between body and soul, outward and inward, which is bad psychology; and also, I venture to think, bad theology. Eye and ear—even touch, taste, and smell—are veritable channels through which our sense-conditioned spirits can receive messages from God and respond to Him.[15]

The sacramental theory of worship is not prominent in American evangelical Protestantism, but this survey of modern worship would not be adequate without at least one mention of its position. The following brief explanation is representative of sacramentalism:

> From the point of view of corporate social worship sacrament and sacrifice are complementary one to the other, or rather are complementary aspects of what is really one act. . . . When we speak of a sacrament we think of that act of God's approach in love and power to the human soul He desires to save. When we speak of a sacrifice we think of that same act as man's response to the love of God.[16]
> . . . Our real need is, in fact, to be more complete and thoroughgoing

---

[14] Comfort, W. W., "The Friends' Theory of Worship." *The Christian Century,* March 19, 1930, pp. 366, 367.
[15] Underhill, Evelyn, *op. cit.,* p. 4.
[16] Streeter, B. H., Editor, *Concerning Prayer.* "The Eucharist," p. 309, C. H. S. Matthews. Macmillan & Company, Limited, 1916.

in our sacramentalism; so to worship Him that we may become more completely inspired by the sacrificial Spirit.[17]

"*Subjective*" *Theories of Worship*

The inadequacy of certain word-labels to designate great movements of thought is seen clearly in the use of the word "subjective" to describe the types of worship which follow. Pratt calls the Catholic mass objective and the Protestant service subjective. But we should fail to understand Protestant worship, as Professor Pratt would agree, if we were content to call it subjective and leave it at that. The theories of worship presented under the heading of "Objective Theories" were all Protestant, and, as was evident, most of them were concerned with the subjective effects of worship. The distinguishing point between these two points of view, as used here, is this: objective worship is worship considered as man's humble duty to glorify an objective and supernatural entity called God; subjective worship is worship which, regardless of theistic theories, has for its final goal the well-being of man, individually or collectively. As explained before, to define these terms one must define them rather close to their extremes. In actual practice, men are found at many points on a scale between them.

The direction or trend of the latter type of worship has been clearly stated by Professor A. Eustace Haydon of the University of Chicago. In an address entitled "Spiritual (Religious) Values and Mental Hygiene" delivered in May 1930, Dr. Haydon says:

> . . . Spiritual values are always human values, and religion is man's age-long quest for these values as an ideal of life-fulfillment. All else in the religious complex—gods and ceremonies and institutions—is merely a means to the desired end—the realization of the good life.[18]

The impatience of one who is inspired with this theory of worship is forcefully asserted by Professor Coe:

> . . . The churches pray, exhort, instruct, but all this is effective, for the most part, only with sins that already lack social standing. Current religion does not know how to deal with the deep depravity of our respectable faults, and indeed it scarcely recognizes them as faults. On the other hand, it magnifies petty virtues and a-dynamic goodness.

[17] *Ibid.*, p. 316.
[18] Haydon, A. Eustace; p. 1. American Foundation for Mental Hygiene, Inc., 1930.

It offers emotional elevation and a sense of selfhood through worship, but since God is rarely worshipped as a creative power here and now at work within the moral order, the worshipper's self remains complacent and accommodating, an arrived and secure soul; it does not become a chrysalis breaking from its shell. Any adequate religion will call for a different way of paying respect to the Creator, and a different way of receiving him into our lives. . . .[19]

Probably no one in our generation continues to insist more emphatically and more logically that worship ought to be contributing to the realization of the social gospel than Professor Coe. In his "charter" for the religious education movement, his *A Social Theory of Religious Education*, he says:

Christian worship is thus realization of the democracy of God—realization by imagination, by fresh insights, by rectification of purposes, by the coincident consciousness of God and our fellows—nay, the interfused consciousness of them, the consciousness of God here and now incarnating himself in us as a society. When worship is fully Christian it is fellowship through and through, fellowship freeing itself from all restraints, and therefore continuous with everything in the world that makes for brotherhood.[20]

The tendency among liberal specialists in religion is to regard worship either as a celebration of the love of life or as a means of untangling the mass of conflicting elements in life. These two purposes are not at all separate in the minds of most of those who hold them, it appears, but they are usually stated separately. Dr. R. C. Cabot, who holds that worship is one of the four things which "men live by," combines these elements in this description of worship:

Worship renews the spirit as sleep renews the body. Our souls as well as our bodies get drained, now and again, of available energy. . . . The tired spirit finds a waning interest in familiar tasks; even contempt may be bred by this ingrowing familiarity. What's the use? What is it all for? we ask ourselves. . . . "Worship is the self-conscious part of the natural recovery of value" in life, when it has grown stale. For worship is the conscious love of the Spirit of the Universe, and we need it regularly like food or sleep.[21]

---

[19] Coe, George A., *The Motives of Men*, p. 211. Charles Scribner's Sons, 1928.
[20] Coe, George A., *A Social Theory of Religious Education*, p. 95. Charles Scribner's Sons, 1917.
[21] Cabot, R. C., *What Men Live By*, pp. 271, 273. Houghton Mifflin Co., 1914.

Professor Charles A. Bennett of Yale University, insisting that "the motive of worship is not moral," says:

> ... I should say that the trouble with the life of action to which worship is the corrective goes far deeper than any mere forgetting of the ends of conduct. ... For our discomfiture is simply this: we have fallen out of love with our world.[22]

An interesting analysis of worship appears in *Modern Worship* by Von Ogden Vogt. His previous work, *Art and Religion*, prepared the way for great interest in the second book in which he explained his theory of worship for our day:

> ... To be in love with life, to have a zest for life, to find it good, to love not merely this or that partial good, but to love life, all of it, to love God, this is religion.
>
> ... Worship is the interruption of work to celebrate. Celebration is achieved in forms of praise and festivity and communion.
>
> ... Worship is essentially the praise and celebration of life. ... This is the abiding element in religion.[23]

Edward Scribner Ames, pastor for years in the same college community which Dr. Vogt serves, analyzes the reasons why men worship and reaches a conclusion somewhat similar:

> God is the Spirit of the world of living beings, taken in their associated and ideal experience. God includes the so-called material world which is the stage of their action and the condition of their existence, and God signifies also the order of their intelligence and conduct. He is the grand total, living process, in which they live and move and have their being. Men cherish this corporate life. They celebrate it in their hymns, in their ceremonials, and in their sense of ideal companionship.[24]

Worship as a method of mental hygiene has been inferred already in this chapter. Recent writers, in harmony with the increasing attention being devoted to the subject, tend to phrase their theories about the purpose of worship more and more in psychological language, or at least in psychological thought.

---

[22] Bennett, Charles A., "Worship in Its Philosophical Meaning." *The Journal of Religion*, September 1926, pp. 489, 490.

[23] Vogt, Von Ogden, *Modern Worship*, pp. 7, 12, 19. Yale University Press, 1927.

[24] Ames, E. S., *Religion*, p. 134. Henry Holt & Co., 1929.

Here are three samples of the consideration of worship from the standpoint of mental hygiene:

> We have whole masses of experience accumulating throughout our whole lives. These experiences are more or less chaotic and conflicting and harmful to our welfare until they are so ordered and shaped by habit as to be helpful to all that we undertake. Worship is the way to organize this totality of experience in such a way as to achieve adaptation to the most vital and potent factor in our environment. . . . Worship is the way we establish that system of habits which is so adapted to the total environment as to catch the supporting lift and movement of this most helpful phase of our total environment—God.[25]

> No, worship is not an escape from the world. It is a preparation for the world, a periodic preparation. It recognizes that "the world is too much with us," that "getting and spending we lay waste our powers." So it takes us aside to straighten out the tangled conflicts of our inner lives and to give us a new sense of poise and uplift. But then it thrusts us back into life again, saying, "Sail on! you must still sail on!"[26]

> Considered from the educational point of view, probably the best objective of chapel is to enable the student to stand aside from the routine of college duties and activities, and to get something of a fresh view and a clearer perspective of the unity of life.[27]

Summary

While there are many gradations of belief between these extremes, it appears from the study above that the two outstanding positions with regard to worship are the traditional theistic and the humanist or near-humanist which claims not to be atheistic. In the first position worship depends upon relationship with God, supernaturally understood; in the second position worship consists of experiences which are beneficial to the individual worshiper and to the social whole, regardless of whether or not God is considered as a part of the experience. The first position is inclined to consider worship the duty of man toward his Creator, while the other begins usually by stressing the values of worship to the worshiper

---

[25] Wieman, Henry Nelson, *The Wrestle of Religion with Truth*, p. 70. Macmillan Co., 1928.

[26] Smith, Robert Seneca, *If Worship Meant Something to Me*, p. 15. Association Press, 1930.

[27] Leonard, Evenden, and O'Rear, *Survey of Higher Education for the United Lutheran Church in America*, Vol. I, p. 366. Bureau of Publications, Teachers College, 1929.

and the effect upon his consequent conduct. The cleavage, however, is not so much about the ultimate effect of worship on the worshiper as it is about the fundamental purposes in worshiping. One might say, if he were willing to risk superficiality in a brief summary, that the first theory tends to consider worship primarily as a duty; the second to regard it as an opportunity.

This discussion of modern theories of worship should not only help the leaders of college worship to find their own positions of thought but it should help them to understand divergent theories which may be found among their student congregations. The brief outline of theories above is sufficient to raise this question: Is there not a tendency toward a conception of worship which is essentially atheistic? If so, the leader of college worship, being, it is assumed, on the pioneering fringe of civilization, ought to know about it. What is there to be said on this topic?

Present-day positions are stated clearly in this paragraph:

> Two religious postulates stand out in marked contrast today. One would require, in order to make experience "religious," that the individual come into helpful relations with God or with one of his revelatory intermediaries (the Bible, Jesus, the Holy Spirit, in conversion, prayer, worship, or in some other striking occasion, such as in sickness, or in the face of death). By adoption of the other postulate, the individual may look upon *any* experience as religious in degree as it proves reciprocally beneficial to him and to the social process of which he forms a creative force. The sense of God may or may not be a factor in the experience. Immediacy of life-values is imperative.[28]

One detects a strong tendency toward the second postulate in this argument:

> ... the lesser gods, and the great gods of all religions, are seen to be the life-process itself, idealized and personified. Every god bears the marks of the habits and moral character of his worshippers, and he undergoes the changes and transformations that profoundly affect his people. When they are militant, so is he; when they are peaceful, so is he; when they have a monarchy, he is a monarch; when they become democratic, he becomes friendly, renounces external authority and rules by reason and justice. God is thus shown to be the Spirit of a people, and in so far as there is a world of humanity, God is the Spirit of the world.[29]

[28] Cole, Stewart G., "What Is Religious Experience?" *The Journal of Religion*, September 1926, p. 476.
[29] Ames, E. S., *op. cit.*, p. 132.

Since prayer has been considered the heart of worship by most writers (Hocking, Weigle, for instance), many people wonder what is left for prayer—and worship—if one adopts the viewpoint put forth by Dr. Ames in the quotation above. One attempted answer to the question is found in an article by Dr. John Haynes Holmes which he entitled, "A Humanistic Interpretation of Prayer." In the article he says:

> . . . I define prayer, in its ultimate and highest meaning, as the conscious and deliberate attempt to gain contact with the universe. Or—to put it the other way around—it is the attempt to merge our lives in the life of the whole, and therewith identify ourselves with cosmic destiny.
>
> This is prayer as viewed from the psychological, the humanistic standpoint. From beginning to end, it is an experience within ourselves. If it is directed to the attainment of ends beyond ourselves, this is only because no man "liveth unto himself." But the prayer process is a human process, a normal process, a natural process.[30]

But many readers of the article, as letters from them later testified, wondered whether prayer as defined in the first paragraph above is really "humanistic." Dr. Ames has this to say about prayer:

> The common conception assumes that prayer implies on the part of the one who prays an idea of a personal God to whom prayer is directed. Such an idea may be present, but to assume that it necessarily is present overlooks those types of religion which lack a clear idea of a personal God and yet employ prayer. . . . Such is the case with the ancient and far-spread religion of Buddhism. . . .
>
> Prayer as here stated is the direction of thought and affection toward those ideal selves and persons that engage the attention of all idealistically minded people. . . . The sense of communion with an ideal personality may strengthen one's morale; it may suggest useful ways of looking upon one's self or the tasks of the day; it may yield the sense of companionship that is so essential to joyous living. . . .
>
> . . . The most realistic expression of prayer is that which occurs within the social group, as in a worshipping assembly, or in an earnest congregation of like-minded religionists. The prayers are indeed addressed to the deity, but to a deity felt to be present in the hearts of his devotees. . . . [31]

But such explanations, and many even more extreme in their views, are not being received with any enthusiasm in many

---

[30] Holmes, John Haynes; in *The Christian Century*, October 16, 1929, p. 1276.
[31] Ames, E. S., *op. cit.*, pp. 207, 212, 213, 217.

quarters. For instance, Douglas C. Macintosh, Professor of Theology in Yale University, says this about the "near-humanist" and the humanist attitudes toward worship:

> . . . Perhaps what is meant is that worship does not require explicit adjustment to God, that any devoted contemplation of ideal values (as being *what* God is—if there be a God) may be regarded as true worship, apart from any belief in the existence of God. . . . No, I have no disposition to deny that it would be possible to use the term "worship" with this meaning. My only question is as to whether it would be worth while to do so and whether we should not be likely to lose more than we could hope to gain by the redefinition. It would enable us to apply the term "worship" to the more idealistic aspirations of the non-theistic humanists, and this might make for pleasant relations between theists and humanists; but would there not be real danger of encouraging the attitude in which nothing specifically religious is valued and no religious experience is sought beyond that meager residue of religion which is still a possibility for the non-theistic humanist? . . .[32]

Dr. F. L. Strickland, Professor of the Psychology of Religion in the Boston University School of Theology, states his position thus:

> Some have maintained that the feeling of awe in the presence of cosmic power, or of admiration and sublimity as we contemplate cosmic order and beauty, are religion. Our answer must be that this is not the sort of attitude-experience which we believe is entitled to the adjective religious.[33]

As Dr. Strickland writes he seems to be pondering over this passage from Pratt's *The Religious Consciousness:*

> . . . There is a kind of worship that is perfectly objective and sincere and that is quite as possible for the intelligent man of to-day as it was for the ancient:—namely that union of awe and gratitude which is reverence, combined perhaps with consecration and a suggestion of communion, which most thoughtful men must feel in the presence of the Cosmic forces and in reflecting upon them.[34]

In reply to this, Dr. Strickland retorts:

> Who could feel *gratitude to a Force?* What does "consecration"

[32] Macintosh, Douglas C., "What Is Worship?" *Religious Education,* December 1930, p. 946.
[33] Strickland, F. L., *Psychology of Religious Experience,* p. 19. Abingdon Press, 1924.
[34] Pratt, James Bissett, *op. cit.,* p. 308.

mean to a Force? What would reverence to or communion with a cosmic Force be like? If the object of worship is thus to be reduced to something impersonal, how can any response be looked for? [35]

The statement has just been made that men in order to worship at all must believe in God. This would seem to be so necessary and obvious that no comment is called for. The history of religious experience taken in relation to the streams of thought about God clearly shows that men do not long continue to pray to a projection of their own ideals. Let God come to be regarded as "an idealized Society" and worship begins to die a perfectly natural death. Of course it is not a sudden death, for habits and customs of very long standing have much social momentum which may keep them going for some time. But the power which will insure the permanence of worship is gone.[36]

The necessity for belief in a personal God in order to worship is argued by Charles A. Bennett of Yale University. He asks, "Must the God of worship be a personal God?" He gives three reasons for his affirmative answer:

> 1. Worship is communion, and it takes two minds to make communion. . . .
> 2. . . . the worshipper is helped. God must come to him from without. It is not possible that he should be revealed by man's effort: He must reveal himself. But no God who is less than personal can do that.
> 3. In worship we not only judge ourselves, we find ourselves judged. . . . A mere ideal is not sufficient to arouse this experience. . . . But a Being who judges us and whose judgment with fear and joy we adopt cannot be less than personal.[37]

In order to complete our picture we must glance at one more conflict in this field. It is between philosophic mysticism and certain aspects of psychology. The position of some psychologists is represented in this sentence from Ames: "It is part of the doctrine of mysticism that the reality with which one seems to be in union, during the ecstatic moments, is the divine Being, though it is also insisted that there is no means of proving to others that the being so found is really God." [38]

[35] Strickland, F. L., *op. cit.*, p. 205.
[36] Strickland, F. L., *op. cit.*, p. 198.
[37] Bennett, Charles A., "Worship and Theism." *The Journal of Religion*, November 1926, pp. 570–85.
[38] Ames, E. S., *op. cit.*, pp. 189, 190.

But all the hinting about the possible delusions of mysticism fails to shake the convictions of genuine mystics. Rufus Jones replies to all such intimations when he boldly declares:

> The main attack in recent years on the validity of mysticism as a religious experience is the characteristic attack of the psychologist. He insists that the experience is purely subjective and consequently lacks objective reference to any reality beyond the individual who has the experience.
>
> We need not blame the psychologist that he tends to reduce religion in all its phases to a subjective basis. He is bound to a restrictive field by the rigid limitations of his science.
>
> There is no more mystery about spiritual Power breaking into and flooding a person's life than there is about electricity breaking through a dynamo, or about ether vibrations coming through a radio set. It is, after all, a question of fact.[39]

Canon Streeter speaks of theism and worship in this fashion:

> Love can only be felt toward persons, and Worship implies a personal God. . . . Personality is the highest thing of which we have experience, therefore it is the least inadequate category under which to think of God. But it is only a symbol. Yet it is a necessary symbol; for to say that God is impersonal is to liken Him, not to the highest, but to the lowest that we know, while to say that He is "supra-personal" may be technically correct, but to the imagination it is meaningless.[40]

It is difficult to say just what is the conclusion to all this, and perhaps the drawing of any conclusion is not necessary. The differing positions remain. No one can know what shifts may be made, nor when, nor by whom. We do know that most of us have assumed that when we worship we must worship something. We have postulated good qualities in the universe, and in worship we have honored the Being who incorporated those qualities into himself and have endeavored to win some of them for ourselves. This theory of worship will surely remain to serve as the background for worship for millions of people to whom it will continue to be serviceable. But it is becoming increasingly evident that for many people the assumption of a friendly and personal

[39] Jones, Rufus, op. cit., pp. 9, 11, 156, 157.
[40] Streeter, B. H., "Worship," op. cit., p. 246.

universe as a framework for worship values will not be serviceable. It is possible that some of the worship of the future will become humanistic without becoming atheistic, i.e., that human values of worship may receive the greater stress. Yet when one examines the moral ideals and the ethical programs of so-called radical groups in religion it becomes apparent that orthodoxy and radicalism are not at opposite poles in these respects. Questions of theism, humanism, and atheism are, after all, very likely questions of method in attaining not unlike ends with regard to the human race. College leaders will probably not wish to shut out of their worship those students who are traveling another religious highway. Can not worship, particularly in college centers, be construed broadly enough to include both those who prefer the mystical approach and those who happen to be skeptical of the supernatural? Is it not possible that the ideal life of man will not be different if it comes as the result of the challenge of the social demands of humanity from that which would come as a result of a heavenly, divine challenge of the Father-God?

B. What Purpose of Worship Is Here Suggested?

The assumption of this portion of the study is that college worship should be planned and conducted in deliberate adaptation to the life and needs of college students. So far as the objectives of college worship are concerned, then, the author of this study agrees with the emphasis of the second theory of worship discussed above, but retains the theistic belief. The underlying beliefs which determine the means of securing these objectives are for the determination of leaders in particular situations.[41] But the general objectives may be more universal in their application. It would be wise for the men and women who prepare and conduct services of student worship to decide in advance the particular aims of each service and then with that aim—or those aims—in mind to plan definitely for their achievement. This means that the leader should adopt very early in his career in the

---

[41] The author conceives of corporate worship as being, for the individual worshiper, a deliberate pause in life for the purpose of appraising values in the experience of life through (*a*) reverence for, or contact or even identification with the highest and best in one's experience (God or one's highest ideals) or (*b*) through devotion to personal excellence in living (Jesus or others) and to a search for help in the attainment of these values through a sense of personal need and a consciousness of spiritual and social comradeship.

field rather definite ideas about the possible accomplishments of worship services and should then proceed to test them with whatever experimentation with his group he feels to be necessary and wise.

In this study the purposes of college worship, the possible outcomes of the worship, have been considered as twofold:

> I. *Ethical:* Through a vision of the ideal and a consequent sense of shortcoming, worship may cause a revision of attitudes and acts.
>
> II. *Appreciational:* Worship should encourage a love of life, a zest for living. In this task worship will attempt such tasks as the alleviation of worry, the promotion of self-confidence, the overcoming of discouragement, etc.

Let us see what this division means when applied to various statements concerning the purposes of worship. It must be understood, of course, that these two objectives are not mutually exclusive. Most services of worship of the newer types may be classified under one or the other, but services very often, perhaps usually, combine the two outcomes. The consciousness of these two main objectives in worship should, however, clarify and focus the work of preparing services of worship. First let us apply these two divisions to the purposes of worship as given by leaders of college worship in their replies to the questionnaire. The purposes of worship are listed here in order of their frequency in the replies and the proper objective is applied to each:

1. To build character: ethical
2. To create and to maintain an interest in religion: appreciational
3. To realize the presence of God and to have communion with Him: appreciational
4. To provide an opportunity for meditation: appreciational
5. To benefit the general life of the college: ethical
6. To help with the day's work: appreciational
7. To help students with personal problems of personality, career, etc.: appreciational
8. To instruct: appreciational
9. To win converts to Christ: either appreciational or ethical

While the appreciational values of college worship appear to be predominant in this list, the weighting of the first item in the list by the large number of replies included in it gives a rather even balance to the two purposes.

Dr. George A. Coe lists seven "ways in which worship can promote the growth of personality." [42] One of the ways is really two ways. Of the eight contributions of worship listed by Dr. Coe five are ethical and three are appreciational. They are listed here according to the twofold division:

Ethical:
1. It can intensify our devotion to a cause. . . .
2. It can include such a facing of our faults as leads to repentance and amendment of conduct.
3. It can save our goodness from over-strenuousness, over-assertiveness, and angularity by making us realize how small we are and how great God is.
4. It can humanize us by fellowship with other worshipers, even those whose worship is much unlike our own, and it can unite a group in support of a cause.
5. It can include a repeated or even a continuous weighing of issues and results, together with sensitiveness to new needs that arise in a changing world.

Appreciational:
1. It can supplant fear, worry, and wearing haste with calm self-possession.
2. By reminding us of central points of view it can promote mental perspective, making great things look great, and small things small.
3. . . . Prevent hardships from taking on exaggerated importance.

Shaver and Stock list "six specific values" which "are to be desired as outcomes of the worship experience." Two of their values are ethical; four are appreciational—the reverse of the emphasis in Dr. Coe's analysis. The six are divided here according to our twofold objective:

Appreciational:
1. There is frequently a deepened conviction of social interdependence.
2. The worshiper often comes from his meditation with a new sense of competence and power.
3. Worship helps the individual to unify his life. Young people are a bundle of conflicting emotions.

[42] Coe, George A., *op. cit.*, p. 123.

4. There is an inner peace which almost certainly accompanies communion with God. . . . The peace which grows out of genuine worship is not that temporary quietude induced by an opiate; it is the reassuring faith which follows upon a season of fellowship with a matchless Friend.

Ethical:
1. Prophetic passion has repeatedly been generated through worship. . . . They are the quiet commitments of honest souls to God's own purposes.
2. Worship helps to create a reverent attitude toward all of life. . . . A right perspective and a proper sense of values should be a fruitage of public worship.[43]

Professor Wieman makes a suggestion which comes close to the theory presented here. He says: "All these ills that result from failure to make proper adjustment to the supreme conditions of a growing life can be summed up under three heads, mental misery, wrongdoing, and impoverished life."[44] Ethical includes "wrongdoing"; appreciational includes "mental misery" and "impoverished life."

The word "appreciation" is not often found in discussions of this function of worship. Shaver and Stock use it in this passage:

> Basic to genuine worship is the attitude of appreciation. This is more important than spoken word or posture. The true worshiper is he who is not cynical toward life, or indifferent to the sequence of events, or merely satisfied to "accept the universe," but who maintains the attitude of gladsome and thoughtful appreciation. Though he speak no word, the spirit of worship dwells within his heart.[45]

The encouragement of a genuine zest for living should be one of the fundamental purposes of worship. It is true that it should not be an uncritical or undirected zest for aimless or useless living. The zest meant here is the very will to live and do and be. This zest, alas, frequently runs low; in some it may be entirely exhausted. If religion has a ministry to the soul and body of man, the building and bolstering of such a will is one of its most important tasks. It can assist in this endeavor if it can help to

---

[43] Shaver, Erwin L. and Stock, Harry Thomas, *Training Young People in Worship*, pp. 19–22. Pilgrim Press, 1929.
[44] Wieman, Henry Nelson, "How Religion Cures Human Ill." *The Journal of Religion*, May 1927, p. 264.
[45] Shaver, Erwin L. and Stock, Harry Thomas, *op. cit.*, p. 15.

resolve those various conflicts which help to destroy peace and happiness. And it will also help if it can build up a wide expanse of appreciations, to help people "to count their blessings, to name them one by one." People need to be impressed with the beauty and worthwhileness of life, its possibilities for heroism, service, and joy. Worship, while not forgetting the evil in the world, should aim to get people to look up, to smile, to be happy, to shake hands—in short, to tackle the adventure of life with an unquenchable zest.

The ethical purposes of worship are being emphasized anew in our day. The favorite line of attack by Christian idealism is against ill-will, particularly racial, national, and religious. Is it not proper to expect that the powerful dynamic of worship should be applied to the intolerances and hatreds of our time?

This division of worship objectives will serve to guide the preparation of services as given in Chapter IV and the collection of materials in Chapter V.

C. What Standards for Guidance in the Preparation and Conduct of Worship Services for Students Do We Need?

Dr. Pratt has stated clearly the practical difficulty in the reconstruction of Protestant worship:

> The problem of reshaping Protestant worship is in fact peculiarly difficult. For it means discovering a method of nourishing the religious sentiments of people most of whom are of the intellectual and active types. And it must do this without the aid of the two most powerful means which other churches and religions make use of for the purpose—namely the kind of belief which makes elaborate objective worship easy and natural for large groups, and a ritual which has the authority and sanctity of generations behind it.[46]

Yet the task of reconstructing programs of worship for college groups, if such worship is not to be discontinued, must be attempted. Many leaders are making such attempts in their own situations, and others, not wishing to risk the turning of indifference into antagonism, will do likewise.

One must realize that, after all, the college chapel is not a church. A college junior wrote to *Religious Education*, saying that "On the whole one might say that the chapel should be a

---

[46] Pratt, James Bissett, *op. cit.*, pp. 305, 306.

church service in moderation."⁴⁷ But not a church service as we ordinarily think of it. The address on the laying of the cornerstone of the University Chapel at the University of Chicago affirms this idea, "The university is in truth not a church, nor is this structure a church or a cathedral."⁴⁸ Not until the leader of college worship is willing to abandon the idea that he is running a church will he be able to gain freshness and insight for his task.

The *assumption* of this study is that a successful program of worship for college students involves a deliberate and definite adaptation of commonly accepted ideas of Protestant worship to the life and thought of students. The following points are intended to show what this means in practice. Some of these standards have a merely "common sense" basis tested with experience; others are deduced from the writings of people familiar with college and religion. They are meant to be of assistance in reaching the objectives before set forth.

1. *The values of the worship period should not be made dependent on religious concepts which are probably doubted or disbelieved by any considerable proportion of the worshiping group.* This has nothing to do with problems of methods of indoctrination. This is not an attempt to avoid meeting or to silence the doubts of students. Dr. Pratt suggests the meaning of this paragraph when he says, ". . . the combination of an inquiring intellect which has not yet got its bearings, and an authoritative religion which insists upon an unreasonable acceptance of dogma is almost certain to breed religious doubt, sometimes of a very painful character."⁴⁹ It is not even the breeding of doubt which is feared, but the loss of a period of renewal of inner strength and peace and the dedication of the self to great purposes. There are many places to discuss the doubts of students; indeed chapel is one of the places. What is here advised against is the unnecessary introduction into the worship period of references and allusions which tend to disrupt the worship spirit of the group and to transform that spirit into one of argument and retort.

2. *The materials of worship should, in the main, assume the aspirations of people who are not unhappy, who have no great re-*

---

⁴⁷ October 1925, p. 362.
⁴⁸ Tufts, James Hayden, "A University Chapel." *The Journal of Religion*, September 1926, p. 450.
⁴⁹ Pratt, James Bissett, *op. cit.*, p. 116.

sponsibilities, who are conscious of no great sin, and who are generally satisfied with life and with their own lives. Professor Wieman suggests these facts when he writes:

> There are three preconditions which must be met before effective worship is possible. The first is that one must go out into deep water. He must take life seriously. He must not shirk the heavy responsibilities. He must venture out to depths where wading is difficult. No one ever worshiped profoundly and with largest results who was not struggling.[50]

Jessie Blount Charters, of Ohio State University, states:

> The religious experience occurs (1) when the human being is caught in a difficulty from which it seems no human power can rescue him; (2) when he is in the presence of a situation which seems to be the gift of divine mercy, since no human power could have produced it to order for him; and (3) when he is the witness of forces seemingly operating under omnipotent control, since no human being could control them without superhuman help, nor could any human being conceivably institute them.
>
> In the first situation we pray for help, for guidance, for mercy; in the second situation we pray a prayer of thanksgiving; in the third we are overwhelmed with awe and worship.[51]

Perhaps we have here the factor which distinguishes the worship of college students from that of grown-ups, and which will account for some of the essential differences in technique employed by the leaders of worship for the two groups. The life of the typical undergraduate is not extremely difficult; it still remains more or less sheltered. Solutions for the greatest problems of life lie not far ahead, but as yet the college student has not gone out into "deep water." Many students are not taking life very seriously. "Heavy responsibilities" are not frequent. "Struggling" is not the word for the average college student. And to go on to Charters' theory, we are not sure that many college students are in any such difficulties, or often think deeply that gifts are of "divine mercy," or are concerned about problems of "omnipotent control." Of course these situations do confront some undergraduates, as advisers know very well; but they are not generally met.

[50] Wieman, Henry Nelson, *Methods of Private Religious Living*, p. 16. Macmillan Co., 1929.
[51] *The College Student Thinking It Through*, p. 25. Abingdon Press, 1930.

The result of this, for many, is a deep-seated conviction of personal adequacy. Life thus far has been so kind that the student can scarcely imagine a situation in which he would not be more than conqueror. He does not come to the college chapel whipped to his knees by the scourge of unyielding life. He comes buoyantly, happily, noisily perhaps, usually laughing and talking with others. And then the leader of the worship wonders why "they" do not appreciate his prayers asking for help in distress, for guidance in confusion, for forgiveness because of sinful living. Too often the leader alone needs the prayers which he offers.

President Ernest H. Wilkins of Oberlin College, in a description of the typical college man which he gave in an address at the Princeton conference on religion in the colleges, said:

> He is in the full vigor of youth, strong, healthy, presuming upon his health, delighting in his own physical ability and in that of his companions.
>
> Things are coming his way. He is going through college, he is getting a good equipment, certain efforts are obviously being made on his behalf, he lives rather well (partly, perhaps, as a result of his own exertions), he has companions, he has plenty of work and plenty of amusement. People like him and he likes people. He's sitting on top of the world.[52]

M. Willard Lampe also confirms this view:

> The world in which students live is a comfortable world. . . . The great majority of the students have plenty to eat and to wear, and lead very protected lives. . . . The world in which students live is a parochial world. . . . The average student really believes that his race, his nation, his state, his university, his fraternity, his particular department of the university are, measured by any reasonable standards, as good as there are.[53]

Professor Edwin H. Byington adds his testimony, saying that for "many young people" their

> desire is that the worship might seem more real: (a) it seems unreal because it assumes a world unlike his. The prayers, the hymns, the anthems largely imply a world of sorrow, suffering, sin, struggle, and disappointment. He has had his share of these, at times more than

[52] *Religion in the Colleges*. Princeton, 1928, p. 6. Galen M. Fisher, Editor. Association Press, 1928.
[53] "The World Students Live In." *Christian Education*, March 1929, pp. 352-61.

his share; but on the whole he finds it a pretty good world in which to live. (b) Similarly the references in worship to human nature make it seem unreal. They recognize mainly two classes. First, those who are bad, thoroughly bad. . . . Second, those who are so pious that they can sing "perish every fond ambition, all I've sought or hoped or known." . . . [54]

Of course this emphasis should not allow the leader of worship to forget the numbers of his congregation whose lives are not fairly easy, but instead are filled with agonies of many kinds. His ministry is to them as well as to the happy.

3. *The materials of worship should not presume too much on the students' intellectual interests, literary knowledge, and acquaintance with the traditional language of religion.* It is well here to note the division among young people indicated by Dr. Coe. He says, ". . . a cleavage is appearing that sets apart two classes among them [modern young people], the conventional (which comprises the vast majority) and the critical (which constitutes only a small, though growing, minority)."[55] Recognition of the existence of this minority group, and recognition of the fact that in nearly all American colleges it is a minority group, will save the leader of college worship from many errors. The greatest of these errors is probably that of mistaking the voice of the critical group for that of the great majority of the student body.

Cyril Harris, formerly Episcopal student pastor at Cornell, writes: "All but the more thoughtful [of the students] are borne along by the tide of custom and opinion, and take things as they come."[56] Professor Robert Cooley Angell gives as the first point in his "General Character of Undergraduate Life" the following:

> The most casual observation of student life will reveal, as it has to so many foreigners visiting our universities, that the general level of intellectual interest among undergraduates is low.[57]

And Professor Byington, speaking of many young people, says: "First, they wish that we would make our worship intelligible to

[54] Byington, E. H., *The Quest for Experience in Worship*, pp. 146–56. Doubleday, Doran & Co., 1929.
[55] Coe, George A., *What Ails Our Youth?* p. 2. Charles Scribner's Sons, 1924. It was interesting at this point to notice a dispatch to *The New York Times* dated February 21, 1931, which reported speeches "by editors of college newspapers of five Eastern universities," saying, "The growing 'conservatism' among undergraduates was a development noted by each of the editors."
[56] *The Religion of Undergraduates*, p. 10. Charles Scribner's Sons, 1926.
[57] *The Campus*, Chap. I. D. Appleton Co., 1928.

them. Organ numbers, Bible readings, words of anthems, theological terms." [58]

The distinction between the critical and the ordinary student should also help the leader to realize that his congregation is not composed entirely of young radicals, or even liberals in any thoroughgoing sense. It is true, of course, that in most colleges of the country the training of the students is in the direction of open-mindedness.

4. *Quoted materials of worship should either be familiar to most of the group or should be easily comprehensible through ordinary oral reading.* It is obvious that poems and prose readings which are not understood have not served the purpose for which they were selected. Because of their condensed nature or the depth of their subject matter some of the finest things in literature are not suited to oral reading, particularly when the attention of the listeners may possibly not be of the most concentrated type. At the same time, quotability should afford no excuse for mere cheapness in materials.

5. *It is well to recognize that the term "God" may have an endless number of connotations to different students, ranging from vague emptiness or complete perplexity to orthodox religious concepts and beyond.* Professor Byington, trying to interpret the young worshiper, says of him: "In addition the presence of God seems almost a fiction, at any rate not a vivid reality. He confesses that he himself is not often conscious of God." [59] The leader of worship will naturally use the term "God" to suit his own understanding. It will be wise for him to consider thoroughly the fact that many young people in his congregation are changing and reforming altogether their notions of God. His use of "God" should not encourage their dogmatic disgust.

6. *The materials of worship should recognize student interest in things modern as opposed to things ancient, particularly when the latter smacks of a solemn piety not felt by the group or savors of unreality in this generation.* Says Professor Angell:

> Undergraduates are also ultra-modern. There is a sophistication about their conversation, a fashionableness about their clothes, an

[58] Byington, E. H., *op. cit.*, pp. 146–56.
[59] *Ibid.*

air almost of condescension toward their elders, which often sets heads of greater experience to shaking.[60]

Cloying piety and assumed sentimentality are out of place in the chapel.

7. *The leader of worship should bear in mind the unsettled nature of students in many ways: vocational, religious, social, sexual, etc.* Themes of worship may arise from this obvious fact.

8. *Worship services should recognize the practical side of the students' religion and at the same time the powerful freedom of modern students by setting forth the needs of modern society which students may help meet.* This interest in the moral and practical rather than the theoretical and orthodox side of religion is affirmed by many educators.

President Wilkins expresses the typical college man's views on religion in these words:

> "Religion is all right—it used to mean a good deal—there's something in it all right—but it simply isn't done, in college. Chapel is a bore. I don't think much of the Y. M. C. A. bunch. And science has proved that a lot of it is all wrong, anyhow. Did you hear what the sociology prof said?" He needs his sleep on Sunday mornings.
>
> And yet, beneath it all and through it all, there runs an undercurrent of unselfish desire to do things that are worth while, to improve conditions on the campus, to improve conditions, by and by, when you get a whack at them, in the city, the country, the world.[61]

Clarence C. Little, former president of the University of Michigan, writes of undergraduate religion in about the same way:

> I do not, for a moment, believe that youth has carefully and conclusively thought this all out. What it feels at present is definite dissatisfaction with the ultra-denominational emphasis of the present-day Christian Church, and the vague urge to accomplish something more honest, more unselfish and more vital in life, than Christianity in its present ritualized form has so far been able to produce.[62]

Professor Angell writes:

> What shall we say of the majority of students who appear uninterested in existing religious institutions? Are they simply irreli-

---

[60] Angell, Robert Cooley, *op. cit.*, Chap. II.
[61] *Religion in the Colleges.* Princeton, 1928, p. 7. Galen M. Fisher, Editor. Association Press, 1928.
[62] *The Awakening College*, p. 266. W. W. Norton and Co., 1930.

gious, or do they arrive at a life synthesis unaided? . . . Perhaps the nearest approach to an adequate statement of the religion of the average student who does not utilize religious forms is to say that he has an embryonic religion but that he is largely unaware of it. Most university men and women believe in living a good life for, as they say, its own sake. If asked to go deeper and examine more clearly the synthesis of which this is an expression, they cannot do it. . . . The future life enters almost not at all into their calculations. In its essence their religion consists in the belief, unconsciously held, that if they live honest, industrious and serviceable lives they will be in tune with the universe.[63]

9. *The leader of worship should very carefully avoid the appearance of attempting to manipulate the group for his purposes, however noble they may be.* Evidence of the mechanics of the service are not only in poor taste, but are disastrous to the spirit of worship. Signals between the organist and leader, or the leader and the person who controls the light switches, are as inartistic as would be a dying actress' motion for the slow curtain. If the leader desires special effects in his services, let him see to it that those who are to assist are well practiced. If that is impossible, then his special plans had better be sacrificed than the service. The result of far-fetched effects in worship services may be as Dr. Pratt says:

> . . . Let him [the worshiper] understand that you wish him to come to church in order that you may make a psychological impression on him, and he will be increasingly likely to stay away.[64]

It may not be trite to say that a spirit of reverence and respect cannot be forcibly imposed on a college congregation nor on any other. A leader may encourage and cultivate such a spirit; he cannot impose it. It should be recognized also that attempts in chapel services to harangue, to shame, or to coerce students with regard to their conduct or their beliefs will probably result only in ridicule or ill-will. Possible distraction from the spirit of worship by the use of students in very prominent ways in the service who may arouse personal or group ill-feeling or jealousy should be considered. Fear of such contingency should not, of course, bar students from frequent participation or leadership in chapel serv-

---

[63] Angell, Robert Cooley, *op. cit.*, pp. 197–99.
[64] Pratt, James Bissett, *op. cit.*, p. 307.

ices. Too little rather than too much such participation is likely to result in the problems mentioned above.

10. *A mean between an unnatural sanctimoniousness and the undignified nature of some religious "pep meetings" will likely be acceptable to most student groups, depending much, of course, on religious background, the type of chapel building and its customary services.* Student love of the beautiful, the colorful, the animate, may well be utilized in chapel buildings, lighting, and order of service. An important feature is mentioned by Professor Byington who says the young person "wishes that the service had more motion, more progression. It seems slow." [65]

[65] Byington, E. H., *op. cit.*, pp. 146–56.

CHAPTER III

HOW MAY WE SOLVE CERTAIN PRACTICAL PROBLEMS IN THE ADMINISTRATION OF CHAPEL SERVICES?

A. Leadership of the Services

The following table shows the titles of the persons who have actual charge of the college chapel services as they were revealed by the questionnaire.

	Private Schools	Public Schools
Faculty members	15 or 22.3%	3 or 20%
President	14 or 20.8%	1 or 6.6%
Chaplain	13 or 19.4%	4 or 26.6%
President or faculty members	7 or 10.4%	1 or 6.6%
President or dean	7 or 10.4%	2 or 13.3%
Dean	4 or 5.9%	0
Faculty and students	3 or 4.4%	0
Visiting speakers (usually ministers)	3 or 4.4%	2 or 13.3%
President and students	1 or 1.4%	0
Clergy and faculty	0	1 or 6.6%
Y. W. C. A.	0	1 or 6.6%
Total	67	15

A total of the various items naming the president indicates that this official is probably the most active in the conduct of chapel services. Various faculty members conduct the services in about the same number of institutions.[1] These figures show also that

---

[1] Faculty members lead about two to one in Dr. A. P. Kephart's report on 392 colleges (*op. cit.*). His ranking was:

Members of faculty	161
President only	88
President or dean	33
Faculty and clergymen	24
Faculty and students	20
Chaplain only	17
Dean only	15

the public institutions tend to employ more chaplains than the private schools, the former using chaplains in more than a fourth of the schools reporting chapel services and the latter in less than a fifth. Taking the two classes of schools in a general total, however, the figures are reversed. Twenty per cent of the private schools returning the questionnaire report the appointment of a chaplain, while only ten per cent of the public schools report a similar officer. The statistics are as follows:

A. Private schools:
  Number not having chaplains   52 or 77.6%
  Number having chaplains   13 or 19.4%
  Number not answering   2 or 3%

B. Public schools:
  Number not having chaplains   31 or 84%
  Number having chaplains   4 or 10%
  Number not answering   2 or 5%

The status of the chaplains in the schools which have them was listed as follows:

A. Private schools:
  Dean of Bible college or theological school   3
  Chaplain only   2
  Head of department of religion   2
  Professor of religion   2
  Professor of religious education   1
  Professor of English Bible   1
  Professor (subject unknown)   1
  Associate personnel director   1
  No answer given   1

B. Public schools:
  Professor of English   2
  Director religious activities   1
  Placement   1

Answers to the question as to who usually delivers the address at chapel were necessarily difficult because there is usually a wide variety of speakers. The following summary is interesting, however:

	Private Schools	Public Schools
Faculty members and various visiting speakers	33	1
Faculty members usually	9	0
Visiting ministers usually	5	3

President usually	5	1
Various visiting speakers	3	0
Chaplain usually	2	1
No answer	10	11

The Work of the Leader

There are many indications that the effectiveness of college worship depends to a surprising degree upon personal factors. Harry Thomas Stock, speaking of students, says, "The minister bulks large in their estimate of the service. More than ought to be the case, he determines their reaction to his own church and, too often, to the church universal."[2] And a college junior, writing to *Religious Education*, says that "the leading spirit should be a man who makes it [chapel] the kind of service to which students will desire to come, a man who, judged by the standards of youth, is a *man*."[3]

The leaders of college chapel services, we learned through the questionnaire, are, in nearly all cases, presidents, chaplains, or other members of faculties. Dr. Henry Sloane Coffin, at the Princeton Conference on Religion in the Colleges, urged continued participation of various faculty members in the chapel services. Said Dr. Coffin:

> . . . Those who conduct prayers must take the utmost pains with both the matter and the language of them. That is not to say that it is wise to confine the conduct of worship to ordained ministers who have presumably received training in the art of leading public services. On most faculties there are devout men with literary gifts who are prepared to give the requisite time and labor to fit themselves to help in this task. They are usually men respected and loved by their students, and the very sight of a man eminent in science, or in literature or in historical knowledge, leading in an earnest service of worship is an inspiration. By all means let us keep as many as possible on our faculties sharing in the leadership of corporate worship.[4]

It is well known that reputation on the campus and impressions made in chapel and out are tremendously important in the work of a college worship leader. A popular leader tends to make a popular chapel.

---

[2] "Church Work with Students." *Christian Education*, April 1930, p. 431.
[3] *Religious Education* for October 1925, p. 362.
[4] *Religion in the Colleges, op. cit.*, p. 21.

The replies to the questionnaire indicate some uneasiness on the part of certain persons replying lest the increasing use of written prayers and many extra-Biblical readings should seem to relieve some of the necessity for the spiritual preparation of leaders. Perhaps there is a danger that the impression may arise that the leadership of college worship is merely a matter of literature and psychology. Leaders themselves should beware of the growth of practices that would give evidence of this. Hugh Hartshorne spoke truly when he said:

> Worship, no matter how skillfully planned, which does not rest back on shared effort or shared emotion may be a useful political weapon, but it is not a highway to God. The leader's duty is one of stimulation and guidance, not dictation or domination, whether by official prestige or personal force of adroitness.[5]

And A. Clutton-Brock elaborates the idea:

> Expression comes of the desire to make spiritual experience complete by making it common. "This has happened to me, but not fully until it has also happened to you." The artist [in worship also] has the eagerness of the child who tells you all about it; if he has not, he is only a proud, dull virtuoso.[6]

The work of the worship leader has been carefully analyzed by Dr. Theodore Gerald Soares, who sees seven steps in the work of the leader. A paraphrase of these seven points follows:

1. Meditation: the beginning of the worship experience in your own soul.
2. Definition: decide on the object and direction of the service.
3. Adaptation: to the level of the particular audience expected.
4. Selection: of the various elements of the service, prayers, music, etc.
5. Preparation: rehearsal, etc.
6. Appreciation: preparation of leader immediately before the service, personal prayer perhaps.
7. Execution: giving attention to details and yet preserving the mood of the worshipper yourself.[7]

---

[5] "Rethinking the Function of Worship." *Religious Education*, December 1928, p. 971.
[6] *The Spirit*, p. 298. B. H. Streeter, Editor. Macmillan Co., 1919.
[7] "The Meaning of Worship." *International Journal of Religious Education*, November 1929, pp. 9, 10.

B. Frequency and Hour of the Services

The following table will show at a glance the number of times per week that chapel is held in many colleges as revealed in several investigations. Successive columns refer to the following:

1. Number of privately controlled schools as disclosed in this study.
2. Number of publicly controlled schools as disclosed in this study.
3. Number of schools as listed in the Kephart report.[8]
4. Number of schools having compulsory chapel as shown in a study privately made by Francis P. Gaines, President of Washington and Lee University (manuscript).
5. Number of schools reporting in the chapel survey number of *Christian Education*, excluding those included in this study.[9]
6. Number of state colleges and universities (10 of 21 studied have chapel services) as shown in Prof. Edward Sterling Boyer's monograph.[10]

Table of Frequency of Chapel Services as Revealed in Studies Listed Above

	1	2	3	4	5	6	Total
Once a week or less	7	6	33	4	1	7	58
Twice a week	5	4	15	3	2	3	32
Three times a week	15	2	29	2	5	0	53
Four times a week	12	3	60	3	3	0	81
Five times a week	26	2	149	5	9	0	191
Six times a week	0	0	46	3	0	0	49
Seven times a week	0	0	5	0	0	0	5
Ten times a week	0	0	2	0	0	0	2

(The total, though undoubtedly containing some overlapping, gives an interesting composite picture of the several studies.)

The table below indicates the hours at which chapel services are held in the schools reporting in this as well as in other similar studies made several years ago. The numbers at the heads of the columns refer to the same sources as used in the preceding table.

[8] Kephart, A. P., *op. cit.*
[9] *Christian Education*, February 1930.
[10] "Religious Education in Colleges, Universities, and Schools of Religion." *Christian Education*, October 1927, pp. 2–6.

Hour	1	2	4	5	Total
7:45	2	0	2	0	4
8:00	0	0	0	2	2
8:15	0	0	2	0	2
8:30	5	1	0	0	6
8:40	4	0	0	1	5
8:45	1	0	3	0	4
8:50	1	0	0	0	1
8:55	1	0	0	0	1
9:00	1	0	3	1	5
9:10	0	0	0	1	1
9:30	2	1	0	1	4
9:45	3	0	0	0	3
9:50	4	1	2	0	7
9:55	0	1	0	0	1
10:00	12	3	7	3	25
10:10	1	0	0	0	1
10:15	1	0	0	0	1
10:20	1	0	3	0	4
10:30	3	0	4	1	8
10:40	3	0	0	0	3
11:00	0	0	5	0	5
11:25	0	1	0	0	1
11:30	2	0	0	0	2
11:40	3	1	0	0	4
11:50	1	0	0	0	1
11:55	0	1	0	0	1
12:00	3	0	5	1	9
12:10	0	1	0	0	1
12:30	0	1	1	0	2
1:00	0	1	0	0	1
2:00	0	1	0	0	1
6:30	0	0	0	1	1

SUMMARY

Chapel Hour	Number of Schools
7:45– 8:59	25
9:00– 9:59	21
10:00–10:59	42
11:00–11:59	14
12 and after	15

The most popular hour for the chapel service is 10 a.m. according to this information. The next most popular hours are 10:30 a.m. and 12 m.

The study reveals that practically all of the privately controlled schools have chapel from three to five times a week, the latter being more frequent than the former. The public schools have chapel less frequently, once or twice a week being the general rule. From the standpoint of improving services, the latter practice seems to offer greater opportunities. The pressure of service following service must be great upon those who must prepare for them and particularly heavy upon those who are trying to do original and careful work.

The popular hours for the service, 10 and 10:30 a.m. and 12 m., appear to have been chosen as the hours when most of the students are about the campus. In most situations the hour of the service is not very important, though in some schools there is considerable agitation about it. If chapel is before classes in the morning, students are tempted to "cut." If chapel breaks up the morning schedule and, attendance being voluntary, only a very few attend, is the interruption justifiable? Is it wise to compete with lunch by using the lunch hour for chapel? A large Eastern university is experimenting with 6:30 p.m. as the chapel hour.

C. The Content of the Services

Part of the questionnaire dealt with the content of college services of worship. It was desired to learn what things are being done to provide a suitable atmosphere and what proportion of the time is ordinarily given to the various parts of the services. Forty-nine separate items were listed by those who returned the questionnaire, giving thirty-three different things which are being done to provide what leaders consider a suitable atmosphere for a college chapel worship service. These items were distributed as follows:

Items Listed as Being Done to Provide Suitable Atmosphere for Devotional Services in College Chapels

	From 49 Replies
1. Organ (or other instrumental) prelude	14
2. Beautiful chapel building or room	6
3. Service entirely religious	6
4. Care taken by leader in the proper conduct of the service	6
5. Processional	4
6. No announcements in the service	4
7. Good devotional speakers	4
8. Student organizations (e.g., Y. M. C. A.) conduct chapel services occasionally	4

9. Special music — 4
10. Attendance voluntary — 3
11. Use of gowns and vestments — 3
12. Use of traditionally religious material (Bible, etc.) — 3
13. Choral or organ responses to prayers, readings, etc. — 3
14. Careful preparation of leader — 3
15. Thought as to posture of worshipers in prayer, etc. — 3
16. Use of a printed ritual — 3
17. Occasional talks about worship — 2
18. Student participation in responses and prayers — 2
19. Periods of silence — 2
20. Nothing but services of worship allowed in chapel — 1
21. Flowers in the chapel — 1
22. Light dimmed at appropriate times — 1
23. Brevity of service — 1
24. Promptness in starting — 1
25. Definite order of service — 1
26. School traditions as to the devotional nature of chapel — 1
27. Regular seating arrangement — 1
28. Closing doors and sending late comers to balcony — 1
29. Organist both a musician and a Christian — 1
30. Preventing distracting noises outside the chapel — 1
31. Faculty sets the example of correct deportment — 1
32. Vary the order of service — 1
33. Memorizing hymns — 1

An attempt was made in the questionnaire to learn something about the total length of the services of worship, about the time usually consumed by chapel addresses, and about the length of the devotional service excluding addresses, when they are customary. The following tables give the information received:

USUAL LENGTH OF THE ENTIRE WORSHIP SERVICE

Minutes	Number of Private Schools	Number of Public Schools	As Given in Kephart's Report
1	0	1	0
12	1	0	2
15	6	1	25
17	1	0	0
20	11	3	24
25	4	1	10
30	19	0	26
35	1	0	1
40	0	1	3
45	1	0	2
60	0	5	2
No answer	19	5	

Usual Length of the Talk in Worship Services

Minutes (Approx.)	Number of Private Schools	Number of Public Schools
3	1	0
5	6	0
7	1	3
10	7	2
12	6	0
15	19	0
20	6	0
30	2	2
No address at all	8	5
No answer	6	5

Usual Length of Worship Excluding Talks Where They Are Customary

Minutes (Approx.)	Number of Private Schools	Number of Public Schools
1	0	1
4	1	0
5	3	0
7	1	0
10	13	6
12	1	0
13	1	0
14	0	4
15	15	0
16	1	0
18	1	0
20	7	1
23	1	0
No answer	18	5

The failure of a large proportion of the leaders to list their efforts to provide a suitable atmosphere for a worship service is significant, for it would seem to indicate that they had done little in this regard of which they cared to speak. Only fourteen mentioned a service prelude, which is the item given most frequently. Only six considered the chapel building or room as helpful enough to mention in this connection. A surprisingly small number mentioned the use of the usual trappings of dignified services—robes, rituals, responses, etc. The impression left with the investigator is that little thought has been given to the provision of a devotional atmosphere for college worship.

The figures giving the amount of time ordinarily devoted to

the various parts of the service are more valuable. They may be summarized here: In the privately controlled schools the entire chapel service usually runs from twenty to thirty minutes, with the tendency decidedly toward the longer time. Ordinarily an address is given which occupies about half the entire time of the service. The leader of the worship service, then, has at his disposal for prayers, readings, music, etc., a period which varies from ten to fifteen minutes. The replies from the state schools on these points are too meager to be valuable, though they seem to show that the services are longer than in the church schools and that the worship period is proportionately shorter.

This study, especially from this point on, is mainly concerned with the use of the ten to fifteen minutes which the leader of the service must plan for. The address, we have seen, is usually given by another person. The wise planning of a brief, compact service for students is the task of the leader in the ordinary situation. This may be the work of a leader five times a week, or, where many have the opportunity, once a year.

D. Music

Music is a part of every chapel service, the replies to the questionnaire indicate. In all of them hymns are sung, and in many there are instrumental preludes as well as an anthem or other "special music." The character of this music should be determined by its purpose.

The general purpose of music in worship has been stated thus by Clarence Dickinson:

> And all this [training in church music] to what end? That through the use of music at once beautiful and appropriate, each service of worship may be skillfully unified into a perfect whole, as the expression of one idea or the illumination of one element or thought in worship, so that the effect of the service may be emotionally intensified and exalted through beauty and through music's direct appeal to the hearts of men.[11]

The important thing about this statement of purpose is that music in worship serves to intensify the unity of the service. Music is

---

[11] Hunter, Stanley A., *Music and Religion*. Introduction by Clarence Dickinson. Abingdon Press, 1930.

not an addition to the service; it is not an extra attraction. It is part of the service. Von Ogden Vogt places this idea of music as its very first requirement:

> First of all, the music of a church service should contribute to its unity. Often it does not do this. The words of the anthems, usually, and frequently the words of the hymns, have little or no connection with the general theme of the service. . . . The next most important manner of regarding music in public worship is its worth as the general matrix of the service. It should be used not only for its own sake, at especially assigned places, but all the way through to bind the parts together. . . . Not only such items as prayer responses, but also short bits of playing while stragglers are being seated or while people are changing their postures, or where the impression of one portion of the service needs for a further moment to be continued or slightly altered before another begins.[12]

The problem of unity is frequently very difficult, especially in the average full-length church service. There, according to Walter Samuel Swisher, "Briefly stated, the problem is to give one mental and spiritual *focus* to a service made up of introductory sentences, invocation, responsive reading, Scripture, prayer (read or extempore), sermon, several hymns, two or more anthems or solos, organ prelude, offertory, and postlude."[13] The problem of the leader of the ordinary college chapel service is easier in this respect because his service is only a fourth to a half as long as the usual church service. There ought to be no excuse in a short service of worship for a lack of fundamental unity. The leader should plan for a short, swift, intense treatment of some worthy theme—much, in construction, like a one-act play. Such unity cannot be achieved without the aid of the musical part of the service.

Unfortunately the improvement of church music has often been interpreted as meaning the mere elaboration of the music. G. Wauchope Stewart combats this idea, saying:

> When I say that our Church music should be the best of its kind, I am not pleading for any elaboration of our musical service. Some of

---

[12] Vogt, Von Ogden, *op. cit.*, p. 176.
[13] Swisher, Walter Samuel, *Music in Worship*, p. 10. Oliver Ditson Co., 1929. This little book should be in the hands of every person having anything to do with "music in worship."

the worst of our Church music is due to the attempt to render something quite beyond the power of the performers.[14]

Professor Byington mentions one reason for this condition:

> ... For nearly fifty years the announcement, "Special Music by the Choir," would increase the attendance, sometimes almost doubling it. ...
> The main function of the music being to attract, selections were made with that in view rather than to enhance the spirit of worship. The music often became an independent feature without any attempt at coördination with the other parts of the service. Often it was not at all worshipful. Sometimes it was a diversion, even a distraction.[15]

The accusations here brought apply mainly, of course, to the choir music, especially the anthem. Writers on the subject feel that it has been hard to bring the anthem into line with the general theme of the service. Von Ogden Vogt says:

> The ambitious and elaborate anthem has its place in the music of the church, but it is greatly overestimated. It is often topheavy with respect to the rest of the service. It is often "lugged in."[16]

Others urge caution in the use of the anthem. George Stewart in his chapter in *Music and Religion* says:

> An anthem cannot have as intimate a meaning for the worshiper as a hymn. ... The anthem should be an acclamation of praise, a meditation, an act of contrition, a direction to adoration; it should never be a musical number, never thrown in hit or miss in a service where it is incongruous.[17]

Walter Samuel Swisher says that "the most worshipful anthem is the simple anthem." Continuing, he says:

> The best church music *for the purpose of worship* is free from unnecessary elaborations. A lovely and effective service may be made up solely of chorales and traditional carols. While the average choir may show contempt for music that is not of a florid and elaborate character, built upon secular models, cultured musicians in our city churches, standing high in their profession, are returning more and

---

[14] Stewart, G. Wauchope, *Music and Church Worship*, p. 79. Hodder and Stoughton, London, 1926.
[15] Byington, E. H., *op. cit.*, pp. 184, 185.
[16] Vogt, Von Ogden, *op. cit.*, p. 177.
[17] Hunter, Stanley A., *op. cit.*, p. 230.

more to traditional music. They do not consider a Bach chorale or a simple motet of the sixteenth century as beneath them. . . .[18]

Dr. Vogt suggests that "where it is difficult, on particular occasions, to find suitable words for the musical part of the service, anthems may be omitted entirely in favor of organ music. . . . An organ number in the midst of the service may sometimes be far superior to an anthem." [19]

Mere unpretentiousness is no virtue, however, as G. Wauchope Stewart intimates when he says:

> . . . However unpretentious the music, it should be solid and dignified in character, free from the emotional gush and cheap sentiment which disfigure so much so-called sacred music, music with a strength and virility about it that make it popular in the best sense of the word.[20]

The number of requests in replies to the questionnaire for assistance of some kind with hymns surely indicates difficulties in this respect in the colleges. The great number of different hymnals used in the colleges reporting indicates also that until recently at least there were few if any outstanding hymnals for college use. A brief consideration of the qualities of hymns appropriate for college use will therefore not be amiss. Weigle and Tweedy did this very thing, only for a younger group, the church school age. They considered the three obvious features: poetry, music, and adaptation to the group which should use the hymns. An outline of the standards which they set up follows:

I. Poetry
  1. Hymns should possess literary merit.
  2. Hymns should be rich in religious values. "If spiritual insight, ethical vitality, and emotional power be lacking, the loveliest of lyrics is not fitted for the purposes of worship."
  3. Hymns should contain true conceptions of God and of our relations to Him.
  4. Hymns should contain wholesome imagery. [Example of the opposite: "There is a fountain filled with blood."]
  5. Hymns should be marked by healthy sentiment. In too many hymns sentiment becomes sentimentality, and feeling a fever. They are effeminate, full of mystical rapture, the

---

[18] Swisher, Walter Samuel, *op. cit.*, p. 38.
[19] Vogt, Von Ogden, *op. cit.*, p. 175.
[20] Stewart, G. Wauchope, *op. cit.*, p. 79.

expressions of a patronizing affection for a "gentle Jesus" rather than the virile worship of the hero of the Gospels.
6. Hymns should be true to life.

II. Music
1. Melody. Is this simple, lyrical, flowing, with no hard intervals, no unusual strain in the range?
2. Harmony. This should be simple but telling, rich but not complicated.
3. Rhythm. This may be marked and often vigorous, but it should be kept free from all irreverent associations.
4. The relation of the music to the thought. Is it a fitting incarnation, a proper medium for the idea's expression.[21]

Most of the standards for the selection of hymns will stand unaltered for college use. The music of the hymns, of course, may be a little more difficult than when intended for younger and less educated singers. Too much must not be expected in this respect, however. Late hymnals for college students often meet objections on the very ground that the students find the hymns difficult to sing. Professor Byington insists on familiarity with the tunes when used in services of worship. He says:

> It is doubtful whether any spiritual impulses are generated in the singing of unfamiliar tunes no matter how good they are. Those who can read music are absorbed in that effort, and feeble participation by the congregation produces depression rather than uplift.[22]

The standards given for the poetry of the hymns are reasonable. Surely students who read the works of the literary masters of the ages in their classes should not be expected to come from those classes to a chapel where literary cheapness prevails. And students who are thinking through their religious beliefs in class and out of class will hardly enjoy the singing of words which are intellectually offensive and spiritually dead to them. George Stewart lists three qualities of good hymns: emotion, vitality, and conviction.[23] Rightly understood, these three qualities would insure good hymns.

More schools reported the use of preludes to their chapel services as a means of providing a suitable atmosphere for worship than any other one thing. Such preludes may be useful

[21] Weigle and Tweedy, *op. cit.*, pp. 35–39.
[22] Byington, E. H., *op. cit.*, p. 182.
[23] Hunter, Stanley A., *op. cit.*, p. 229.

for that purpose, but most of us know that they are not always effective for the simple reason that at times they can scarcely be heard above the talking of the congregation. The organ (or other instrumental) prelude is helpful in fostering the spirit of worship when combined with other factors. The most important of these is the disposition of the congregation to participate in the service; to help and to be helped. Other important factors are the impressions conveyed by the room in which the service is being held, and the conduct of the leaders of the service during the prelude.

The organist's task may be simplified by this one question: Do my preludes tend to foster a spirit of reverence in the congregation? A prelude to a service of worship is not an organ recital. It is not to entertain, not to teach music appreciation, not to startle and amaze. Its sole task is to add to the unity of the service.

The use of an orchestra in the chapel service was mentioned in some of the questionnaires. No one may deny the value of good orchestral music in evoking the worshipful spirit, and, on the other hand, no one may deny the distractions and annoyances of the bothersome orchestra in a worship service. H. W. Gibson says:

> Nothing jars the spiritual nerve of the individual and surcharges the atmosphere with discord as the continual screeching process of "tuning up" indulged in by instrumentalists. An orchestra many times interferes with congregational singing as frequently the attention is directed to the orchestra instead of being focused upon the hymn. . . . Do not employ an orchestra unless it is skilled and practiced and every member enters heartily into the spirit of the service.[24]

And Earl Enyeart Harper says:

> Nothing will so certainly defeat the very end and aim of a congregational service of music and worship as an orchestra out of tune with itself, with imperfect ensemble, overstrong in some sections, especially the brass, and woefully weak in others, possibly so intent on notes and fingering as to be altogether unresponsive to the direction of the leader.[25]

[24] Gibson, H. W., *Services of Worship for Boys*, p. 12. Association Press, 1914.
[25] Harper, Earl Enyeart, *Church Music and Worship*, p. 213. Abingdon Press, 1924.

The ideal service of worship, particularly the short service used in college chapels, should be an artistic unity. Instrumental and choral music, in the hands of an interested and intelligent leader, will assist greatly in the achievement of that unity and of the great purposes of worship.

The following is a résumé of the replies to questions concerning the use of song leaders and various types of choirs in college chapels. The numbers in every case refer to the number of schools employing that practice:

	Private Schools	Public Schools
Music led by a designated song leader	23	9
Music led by the person in charge of the service	15	0
Music led by chorus or choir:	23	9
Mixed choir 19		
Female choir 6		
Male choir 7		
Music led by quartet:	6	0
Mixed 4		
Male 2		
Female 0		
Mixed quartet and designated leader also	1	0
Mixed chorus with designated leader also	2	4
Female chorus with designated leader also	2	2

The findings indicate that the chances are about equal that the music in the chapels will be in charge of a designated song leader (with no choir) or a choir. In nearly a fifth of the church schools the leader of the service is also in charge of the music during the service, presumably announcing the hymns and giving any directions he desires about their singing. It would seem that many of the colleges are in good condition from the standpoint of musical organization to have appropriate and effective music in their chapel services.

Sixty-three colleges report the use of forty different hymnals, while one uses song sheets only and another uses hymn slides thrown on the screen. Only nine of the forty hymnals and song books are used by more than one school. These nine and the number of schools using each are as follows:

American Student Hymnal (Century Co.)	10
A Hymnal of Praise (A. S. Barnes Co.)	5
Methodist Hymnal (Methodist Book Concern)	5
Hymns for the Living Age (Century Co.)	3

Revised Presbyterian Hymnal	2
American Hymnal (Dawson)	2
Cokesbury Hymnal	2
Assembly Hymn and Song Collection (C. G. Hoover)	2
Chapel Hymnal (Pilgrim Press)	2[26]

The fact that sixty-three colleges have forty-two different sources for their hymns, though interesting if not amusing, is not so surprising, considering the vast differences between many of the colleges in many ways, as the obvious range in the level of their hymnals. Hymnals range anywhere from the *American Student Hymnal* and *Hymns for the Living Age* to *Revival Echoes* and *Evangel Bells*. Perhaps even the publishers of the last two would be surprised to learn of their adoption for college chapels. The difficulty, of course, has been that there have been few good hymnals which were designed for college use. Twelve of forty-two requests for materials for college worship received through the questionnaire deal with the securing of suitable hymns. Good evidence of the fact that many college people have been eagerly awaiting the publication of a hymnal planned specifically to meet their needs is the announcement that more than sixty American normal schools, colleges, seminaries, and universities have adopted the *American Student Hymnal*.

E. Silent Worship

Another phase of the improvement of college worship which must not be overlooked is the use of silence in worship. We are accustomed to think of silence as the exclusive possession of

---

[26] The following hymnals are each used by one reporting college:

Assembly Praise Book	Hymns and Prayers
Assembly Songs and Choruses	Hymns of the Christian Life
Association Hymnal	Hymns of Worship and Service
Century Hymnal	Hymns for the Church
Christ in Song	Inter-Church Hymnal
College Hymnal	Joint Synod Hymnal
Episcopal Hymnal	Junior Assembly Song Book
Evangel Bells	Life Service
Goucher College Hymnal	Living Hymns
Harvard University Hymn Book	Parish School Hymnal
Hymn and Tune Book with Services	Pilgrim Hymnal
Hymnal for American Youth	Revival Echoes
Hymnal of the Augusta Synod	Revival Songs
Hymns of the Church	St. Olaf Song Book
Hymns of Praise No. 2	Yale University Hymns

Friends' worship, but there are evidences that others are considering its values. For instance, Dr. Simpson writes:

> Concerning silence in worship, I shall only say this. I feel that in all our Churches to-day, and especially in our Presbyterian Churches, there is too much talking. There is a worship of the soul which is best rendered in silence. There is an acquaintance with God that comes only through stillness. There is a voice of God that is heard only when the soul is waiting hushed for God. Should not this be an integral part in every act of public worship . . . ?[27]

Canon Streeter explains the value of silence in this way:

> The communion of the soul with the Divine necessarily has a reciprocal character; there must be moments of pure receptivity, moments of conscious self-expression. He who would pray must at one time speak, at another listen. . . . Hence intervals of silence in which individuals can think specially of their own or their friends' needs, or in which the whole body is invited simply to wait upon God, are a vital necessity.[28]

From another source comes a testimony of the value of silence. Professor Otto, in his *The Idea of the Holy*, states that Western art has only two direct methods of representing the *numinous*, the non-rational and non-moral element in religion: darkness and silence.[29] And Dr. Stanton Coit says that:

> The period allotted to preconcerted silence at the Ethical Church is always two minutes. . . . Social silence is the revealer not only of the ineffable depth of our own life but of the inner worth of other men. It especially makes palpable the unifying Will, the commanding genius of the social group to which we belong. The spirit of the fellowship which has made the many one now spreads its pinions with gentle might over and above us, and makes itself felt as an all-enfolding presence, quickening and consoling us. Therefore to all Modernists is to be commended the discipline of social silence as an essential item in public worship.[30]

The committee on worship of the Princeton Conference on Religion in the Colleges included this in their report:

---

[27] Simpson, Robert S., *Ideas of Corporate Worship*. T. & T. Clark, Edinburgh, 1927.
[28] Streeter, B. H., *op. cit.*, pp. 266 and 270.
[29] Otto, Rudolf, *op. cit.*, p. 70.
[30] Coit, Stanton, Editor, *Social Worship*, p. xxv. West London Ethical Society, 1913.

There is room for an increasing use of silent worship. Most of the group confessed a lack of satisfaction in "creative silence." Without doubt, preparation for such worship is as important as it is rare, but it is worth working for it.[31]

This committee was evidently doubtful of the methods of conducting silent worship for college groups, and they may well be. The awful boredom which resulted in some attempts at silent worship may have been in their minds. "Silent worship," says L. Violet Hodgkin, "at its worst is probably as artificial as the most ornate ceremony, and is possibly even less profitable to the soul." And she continues, in her Swarthmore Lecture, to quote Charles Lamb, "More frequently the Meeting is broken up without a word having been spoken. But the mind has been fed. You go away with a sermon not made with hands. You have bathed with stillness." And she adds, "To the Quaker, the silence in his worship must be free, and not compulsory. There must always be full liberty to speak."[32] How to achieve all these ends without getting silent worship "at its worst" is the leader's difficulty when he plans for his group to worship silently. Cyril Hepher gives a "secret" of such worship. He says:

> The blending of silence with fellowship seems to create an atmosphere in which the sense of the spiritual in man is set free. . . . Here was this neglected art in practice without the sense of baffling difficulty. What was their secret? They were doing it in *fellowship*. . . . Men who being all in one place, and all of one mind, seek God in the silence side by side, draw from their companionship a force which gives the soul new power.[33]

Leaders of college worship, thinking of the possible application of silent worship to their own groups, may smile at the thought of such "seeking" during the assembly of the entire school or a large part of it. Silent worship, it would seem, is much easier for small groups than for large heterogeneous groups, many of whom, if not hostile, are surely not very much interested. Yet no one can deny the worship values of "social silence," and many are trying it in some form. The commonest way is the directed or guided prayer of meditation. In such an exercise, the leader states a

---

[31] *Religion in the Colleges*, p. 58.
[32] Hodgkin, L. Violet, *Silent Worship*, pp. 63, 61. Swarthmore Press, 1919.
[33] Hepher, Cyril, Editor, *The Fellowship of Silence*. Macmillan Co., 1917.

topic for meditation and a brief period of silence follows. Appropriate organ music may help considerably to maintain the spirit of worship and to fill up the gap which some in the group may feel. Later even this may be omitted, if it seems best, and absolute silence may occur during the brief intervals of silence between the prayers or Scripture lesson or other helpful reading which the leader may be using. Many young people are familiar with periods of "silent prayer" before they come to college, for such periods are fairly common in young people's religious meetings. This experience should be valuable to the leader as he plans to extend the idea of silent worship.

CHAPTER IV

HOW MAY WE PREPARE ACTUAL SERVICES OF WORSHIP FOR CHAPEL?

A. EXPLANATORY

1. *The Question of Ritualism*

The increasing use of ritualism, liturgical forms, symbolism, is obvious in American Protestantism, though the movement has not gone to extremes in many places. Chapel leaders who are eager to dignify and enrich their services often turn to the use of ritual. What is its value?

"It is evident," says Professor Byington, "that, outside the realm of religion, all Americans use symbols freely." And, in a memorable passage,[1] he refers to the raised hat, the handshake, the kiss, flowers, pins, rings, flags. He refers also to the use of vestments in lodges and in academic circles. He speaks of the pride of lodge people in their "wonderful ritual." He points out the ceremonialism surrounding young life in the oath of allegiance to the flag and in organizations like the Boy Scouts and in pageantry everywhere. "A generation is growing up," he concludes, "accustomed to symbols, forms, and rituals; and it likes them."

The president of a well-known college, in a letter accompanying the questionnaire, said, "I might add that in our chapel service we adhere to a rather severe simplicity and the utmost dignity. We find the students desire the latter quality especially. . . . The choir and preacher are gowned, and we are gradually developing a touch of ritual in the service." This is from a mid-western Presbyterian college. As was noted before, the requests for materials indicated an interest in increased ritualism.

Harry Thomas Stock, prominent worker with young people, reports:

> Some students (without regard to denominational upbringing) desire the religious experience which comes from a liturgical service.

[1] Byington, Edwin H., *op. cit.*, pp. 23–25.

Others are impatient with what they think of as the trappings of such a service, and want only a sermon.²

And Professor Soares says that "Perhaps all might be benefited by the use of both the ritual and spontaneous worship.³ There are many, of course, who are frankly afraid of the use of ritual. They fear that its non-intellectual approach to religion will tend toward stagnation and toward abuses of the powers of suggestion. The mere cry of "popery" no longer causes convulsions of terror in informed circles; better arguments must be advanced. But there is much to say for the new interest in ritualism. Von Ogden Vogt writes:

> In the more restricted sense, ritual is very powerful. . . . I know that this is precisely the reason why many people do not wish to use ritual. They fear that it is too powerful. Yet, at the same time, they go about hunting for something else that will be powerful enough to interest and hold the youth. It is surely absurd, on the one hand, to bewail the devices for holding the young and, on the other hand, fail to use an admittedly powerful instrument for it.⁴

"The present generation of students," says the president of Union Theological Seminary, "is more sensitive esthetically than were their predecessors thirty years ago. They appreciate architecture, music, literary form; and a service of worship ought to be conducted under the most favorable circumstances." ⁵

> Its function [ceremony] as we have seen, is to prepare the mind to worship, to put the individual in that state of mind in which he is able to perceive God. That means that the jammed doors of the mind must be wedged open so that the fullness of experience may stream into the field of awareness and thus make God perceptible to the worshipper.⁶

The danger in the amateur's use of ritualism may lie in the artlessness of his art. Eager to have beautiful services of worship, to conduct more and more elaborate services with more and more assistants to manage various items in the "devotional

---

² "Church Work with Students." *Christian Education*, April 1930, p. 431.
³ Soares, Theodore Gerald, *A Dictionary of Religion and Ethics*, p. 417. Macmillan Co., 1921.
⁴ *Modern Worship*, p. 108.
⁵ Coffin, Henry Sloane; speech reported in *Religion in the Colleges*, p. 21.
⁶ Wieman, Henry Nelson, *Religious Experience and Scientific Method*, p. 55. Macmillan Co., 1927.

atmosphere" provided the amateur may allow the manipulation of the service to destroy the service. As Von Ogden Vogt says:

> They [the people] should get the effect without being called upon to notice the management that produces it. It is easy for the planners of public exercises to produce an artificial effect. This is the risk of all analysis and all painstaking. But the lack of analysis and of painstaking has in many churches brought about usages which are ugly and unendurable to larger and larger numbers of people. . . .[7]

One of the commonest practices of modern non-liturgical worship has been the use of formal, or written, prayers. Most of the Protestant books of worship contain such prayers. Like the use of printed hymns, such prayers, varied from service to service usually, prove a feature of liturgical worship acceptable to most other groups. As Professor Conklin says:

> A distinction has been stressed between spontaneous and formal prayers; but such a distinction, so long as the motive remains that of desire for religious experience (communion with God), is more literary than it is psychological. To be sure, the literary difference is often very great. Any one who reads the beautiful formal prayers of the Bible or the better known prayer manuals, and compares them with the crude utterances so often heard from many pulpits, cannot fail to recognize a difference which is both notable and pitiable.[8]

The usual tendency of extemporaneous prayer was pointed out in a doctor's dissertation at the University of Chicago years ago:

> Extempory prayer, which, as is well known, is to take the place of the form prescribed in liturgical churches, is itself in danger of following definite grooves. The individual, through repetition, becomes familiar with a particular sequence of thought and says his prayer as automatically as though he were reading it out of a prayer book for the thousandth time. The churches that started out with a lively protest against the dead ritual have manifested a constant tendency to adopt definite forms of worship.[9]

Not only is there an increasing use of written prayers, but the movement against the "long prayer" is growing. Many con-

[7] *Op. cit.*, p. 165.
[8] Conklin, Edmund S., *Psychology of Religious Adjustment*, p. 181. Macmillan Co., 1929.
[9] Henke, F. G., *A Study in the Psychology of Ritualism*, p. 87. University of Chicago Press, 1910.

tend that the attempt to lump together all the elements of prayer in one long prayer is not often effective in public worship. Professor Pratt makes this typical observation:

> How many of the congregation are praying in any real sense of the word during the "long prayer" is a question which only He who hears prayers could answer. If I may trust my own observation, and the expressions of those whom I have questioned upon the subject, no very large portion of the congregation "follow" the long prayer, and fewer still find it really helpful in producing even the prayerful attitude of mind.[10]

2. *The Order of Service*

The first two conclusions to Dr. Kephart's survey of college chapels [11] are these: (1) Many schools are experimenting to improve chapel exercises. (2) The great variation in plans, programs, and general procedure indicates that there is no one solution. He lists seven different orders of service which typify practically all the chapels which replied to his inquiry. The most common order is this: song, Scripture, prayer, talk, announcements, song. The other six orders differ from the first chiefly in the use of the Lord's Prayer, the Doxology, or the Gloria Patri.

The present investigation did not call for the securing of an order of worship from the schools listed, but the questionnaire did state that such programs would be appreciated. Twenty-three schools sent a detailed order of their week-day chapel services, and several others gave the order of the Sunday worship. We are here interested mainly in the briefer service of the week-day. The Sunday services tended to be more formal than the week-day, to be longer, and to have addresses of ordinary sermon length.

All the week-day chapel services contained a hymn and some form of prayer, but beyond that there was no agreement. The following interesting list shows the frequency of the elements listed in the twenty-three services reported in detail:

Address	12
Call to worship:	10
By leader	4
By leader and congregation	3

---

[10] Pratt, James Bissett, *op. cit.*, p. 302.
[11] Kephart, A. P., *op. cit.*

By choir	2
By leader and choir	1
Prelude	10
Scriptural responsive reading	9
Lord's Prayer in unison	6
Anthem or special music	5
Unison prayers (excluding Lord's Prayer)	3
Chants:	7
Gloria Patri	3
Doxology	2
Others	2

One school listed "Check on Attendance" as one step in their service of worship. We can not afford to generalize on the basis of these few orders of service, but a comparison between these facts and Dr. Kephart's (of six years ago) shows (at least in these schools—which are believed to be representative) a tendency toward some little "enrichment" of the services. This is particularly noticeable in the "Call to worship," which was listed by nearly half the schools.

One of the findings of the section on Corporate Worship of the Princeton Conference on religion in the colleges was:

> A mélange of hymns, prayer, talk, college song, and announcements may be the inevitable combination for an assembly, but it cannot be effective in worship. A service of worship must have unity and dignity.[12]

These are the qualities in worship which leaders everywhere are striving for. It is becoming customary for services to have themes and to be planned for a careful development of these themes.

Dr. Vogt lists these "laws of form in the arts generally" which he applies to the art of worship:

1. Singleness, unity, wholeness
2. Movement (sequence and a climax)
3. Rhythm (processionals, responsive readings)
4. Design [13]

The first of these laws of form, then, is unity. Such a principle for worship is adopted by most present-day leaders. This principle, however, requires understanding. For instance, we find Dean Sperry saying, "We may safely say, then, that a service of

[12] *Religion in the Colleges*, p. 58.
[13] Vogt, Von Ogden, *op. cit.*

worship conceived in a single mood and confined to a single idea will be monotonous."[14] But unity should not mean monotony, for monotony would destroy worship. Canon Streeter observes, "No student of the psychology of attention is surprised to find that experience teaches that a congregation which is 'bored' simply *cannot* worship."[15] Indeed, unity should be the cure for monotony. The unity of theme will bind together the various parts of the service while the variety of moods will insure progression and interest. Dr. Sclater achieves this variety in his "principle of alternation." "Inevitably, he [the worshiper] will tend to swing from the thought of the holiness of the worshipped, to the unworthiness of the worshipper. . . . He will move rhythmically between Vision and Response."[16] Dr. Vogt achieves it in the variety of his seven steps in worship. Dean Sperry achieves it through his division of worship into thesis, antitheses, and synthesis.

The important rule to follow in achieving unity through a variety of moods is that stated by Canon Streeter:

> . . . the guilding principle should be "one thing at a time"; and those parts of worship which demand the greatest concentration should be broken up by intervals. That is to say, confession, thanksgiving, petition for personal needs, and intercession for others, should not be combined in one long supplication; they should be divided from one another by the other and less exacting elements in the service, such as hymns or scripture reading. And not only that, but whenever in any of these divisions the congregation is to be invited to pass from one subject to another the change ought not to be sudden, unexpected or hurried.[17]

The principle of "movement" is important if a service of worship is to have practical as well as artistic effectiveness. One part should follow another in logical fashion, and the service at some central point should reach a climax. This climax may be a creed, a hymn or a prayer of dedication, the offering, or a communion service, depending upon the purpose of the service. Without this element of dedication to new or renewed ideals a service of worship fails to arrive.

[14] Sperry, Willard, *op. cit.*, p. 281.
[15] Streeter, B. H., *op. cit.*, p. 266.
[16] Sclater, J. R. P., *op. cit.*, p. 25.
[17] Streeter, B. H., *op. cit.*, p. 287.

One of the aims of most worship leaders of to-day is for the increased participation of the congregation in the service. Replies to the questionnaire indicated considerable interest in the use of unison prayers, litanies, responsive readings, etc. The person who conducts a service of worship is not an entertainer nor is he merely worshiping publicly; he is leading a group of worshipers in united devotions.

The principle of "design" is often difficult to work out. In many places the design or plan of the services has been fixed by tradition. But more frequently the leader has more or less liberty in planning his own service. In that case he will probably want to follow the recommendations of the Princeton Conference committee on worship:

> The experimental approach was emphasized. It is a mistake to be bound to traditional forms and methods in the chapel work. There is a wealth of new material now available, new rituals, new musical forms, new books of prayers, volumes of selected readings from great prose and poetry. Chapel leaders should draw on this fresh literature of worship. . . . There is a need for richness and variety in the services in order to satisfy the needs of persons with different religious background.[18]

A proper plan for each service is difficult to achieve, particularly when the materials and purposes of the services may be unusual. Yet this "putting together" of the elements of the service in a convenient, artistic, and effective manner must be attempted. To assist those who are engaged in such attempts, a variety of modern orders of service will be listed here. Some of them may serve as models or forms for chapel services.

The plan of Professor Wieman may furnish a plan for the consideration of problems in worship services. It has three parts: exposure to God, diagnosis, and reconstruction. The first is an exposure through scripture, etc., to that which the worshiper "believes to be of greatest concern to human living." This, he says, is what our fathers called praise and adoration. In diagnosis "we must find out wherein our habitual adjustments are inadequate for realizing those possibilities which the environment has in store for human living. . . . Our fathers called it confession of sin." In reconstruction, the worshiper "forms as clear and

---

[18] *Religion in the Colleges*, pp. 58, 59.

definite concept as he can of what is required of him, in the form of readjusted attitude to correct the faulty habit and enable the environment to accomplish what is desired. Then he states this required adjustment of habits in words as comprehensive, accurate, concise and forcible as possible. . . . Always this statement of need should be in the affirmative, not negative, language." [19]

There are many variations and restatements of this order of worship. For instance, Kagawa, in an interview reported in the *Christian Century*, gives three steps in "the way of meditation: rest, emptying of the soul; reflection, repentance, confession"; and "living up to God—prayer, the incarnation of love through action." [20] Dean Sperry's plan for worship is similar:

1. Adoration of attribute of God
2. Definite contrast of man with God
3. Assurance of forgiveness
4. Rededication of self[21]

The idea of initial adoration followed by the humility of confession is included in Von Ogden Vogt's scheme of liturgical form, which is often not understood when only the seven key words are quoted:

> Introduction: Call to worship or preparation (invocation, exhortation, Scripture verses. May indicate theme of service.)
> 1. Vision (presence of divinity is invoked or celebrated.)
> 2. Humility (The first reaction to the vision of God is the spirit of humility in man.)
> 3. Vitality (praise and rejoicing for the floods of vitality)
> 4. Recollection (the major mental and moral content or worship; prayers, litanies, scriptures.)
> 5. Illumination (the expression of convictions)
> 6. Dedication
> 7. Peace (closing hymns and benedictions)[22]

Weigle and Tweedy have most of this in their fivefold plan for worship: adoration, confession, thanksgiving, supplication, sub-

---

[19] Wieman, Henry Nelson, *The Wrestle of Religion with Truth*, pp. 71–74. See also Professor Wieman's analysis of private worship in his *Methods of Private Religious Living*, pp. 22–30.

[20] Brown, Ina C., "Kagawa Diagnoses American Religion." *The Christian Century*, September 24, 1930, p. 1147.

[21] Sperry, Willard, *op. cit.* A summary of material presented on pp. 282 ff.

[22] Vogt, Von Ogden, *op. cit.*, pp. 49–52 (selected passages).

mission.[23]   G. A. J. Ross, with one substitution, uses these same elements in a slightly different order: adoration, thanksgiving, confession, affirmation, self-devotion.[24]

An order of worship which has many suggestive points is the one presented by Dr. Sclater.[25] After each point in his outline will be found a note designed to explain the elements in the service to carry out the ideas:

I. Approach or Preface
    1. The call to worship (Come, let us worship)
    2. The realization of God's presence (The Lord is in his holy temple)
    3. Cry of help or invocation (Almighty God, unto whom all hearts are open)

II. The Worship
    4. Adoration (Hymn, most likely)
    5. Prayer of confession, and for pardon, cleansing, and peace
    6. Expression of the moral law (sung or read)
    7. Prayer for aid (Anthem or hymn)
    8. God's compassion (Scripture)
    9. Thanksgiving (Doxology, TeDeum, prayer, or hymn)
    10. The Intercessory Prayer ⎫
    11. Lord's Prayer ⎬ Climax
    12. Offering—with dedication sentence ⎭
        (Benediction, if desired)
    13. Appropriate transitional hymn to sermon
    14. Sermon
    15. Quiet dismissal hymn
    16. Benediction

Dr. E. S. Conklin, Professor of Psychology at the University of Oregon, publishes an order of service in use at the First Presbyterian Church of Portland which he thinks "closely approximates that which is psychologically ideal." The exact order will not be reprinted here, but Professor Conklin's analysis of it is worth reprinting:

> The entering impression was well supplemented by the prelude, the invocation, and the hymn of praise, and all combined stimulated thoughts of the presence of God and that complex emotion of awe which is analyzable into inferiority, wonder and some infusion of fear.

---

[23] Weigle and Tweedy, *op. cit.*, p. 13.
[24] Ross, G. A. J., *op. cit.;* a summary of the discussion on pp. 31–37.
[25] Sclater, J. R. P., *op. cit.*, pp. 53–54.

Then the confession followed. It is psychologically the first step toward the new adjustment phase of the religious experience. This past was completed by the assurance of pardon and the hymn of consecration. The next items led up to the prayer of intercession supplemented by the silent prayer (necessitating active participation on the part of the worshiper) and the Lord's prayer, the items of which reviewed what had preceded. The consciousness of forgiveness and of new adjustment normally involves the arousal of tenderness, not only toward God but also toward mankind, a most significant part of that world to which the new adjustment has just been made. This new kindliness as well as the new adjustment finds expression and emphasis in all of the remaining items of the order.[26]

Dr. Hartshorne's article on "Rethinking the Function of Worship"[27] is relevant here. His theory coincides somewhat with the outline of Dr. Wieman with which this section began. Worship according to Hartshorne's scheme, has three parts: "unification and establishment of appropriate 'sets' for worshiping together; presentation of situation and its revaluation; and crystallization of attitude in some appropriate expression and in forward looking social purpose." His order of service, printed in the article, uses also the idea of "contrast between practice and ideal" with the "contrast merging into release and sense of forgiveness and fellowship with God and one's fellows, present and absent" and "connection with subsequent activity."

The services of worship in the following chapter are designed to illustrate the theories of worship set forth on the findings of this study. They endeavor to show how the purposes of worship presented in the first chapter may be worked into actual services; they are planned to conform to the standards for college worship, outlined in Chapter IV; and they are meant to illustrate various orders of worship. Most of the services in Chapter IV follow one or the other of the following orders of worship, both of which borrow heavily from the theories introduced in this section.

ORDER OF SERVICE I

1. Preparation for worship
   A. Prelude
   B. Call to unity in worship

---

[26] Conklin, E. S., *op. cit.*, pp. 186, 197.
[27] *Religious Education* for December 1928.

C. Statement of the theme (in conjunction with B if desired)
2. Adoration of God or of an ideal or a virtue
3. Confession of failure to live up to this high vision
4. Resolution to adjust to the desired goals of life

ORDER OF SERVICE II

1. Preparation for worship
   A. Prelude
   B. Invocation or call to worship
2. Statement of the problem which is the theme of the service
3. Development of the problem, suggesting a way or ways of dealing with the problem
4. Dedication to the adopted solution of the problem

There is no arbitrary place for a hymn, or a prayer, or a poem. Everything must fit into the order of service according to its ability to fit into the scheme. A hymn may serve almost any phase of either of the two outlines above; so may a poem, or a prayer, or a response. These outlines are designed to secure conformity to the "laws of form in the arts generally" as stated by Dr. Vogt—unity, movement, design (with rhythm to be worked out in the further planning of the materials to be used) —and to adapt all this to the worship of college students. Most chapel services are short, and these orders of service may be condensed easily to ten to fifteen minutes. Yet much is gained in directness, simplicity, and progression. Ample use may be made of student-suggested themes, and student committees or joint student-faculty committees may work out services according to these plans.

3. The Selection of Themes for the Services

The use of definite themes in worship services is familiar to all who have any acquaintance with modern worship material, i.e., hymnals, books of services, etc. The resulting concentration of thought in worship is evidently thought to be more helpful than the vague effect of more generalized services. This should be particularly true of the brief (in some cases, introductory) services which the questionnaire showed to be the common practice in college chapels.

This study proposes that the worship themes of college chapels shall be drawn from the life and thought of students. This means that the leaders of college worship can not live without constant contact with the student group and expect to be able to conduct student-centered worship. Indeed, in most situations it means that students themselves should do as much of the planning as is convenient in a coöperative manner.

Suggestions for appropriate themes may come from among the following (no order of importance is intended):

1. Patriotic occasions which naturally awaken student interest.
2. Special religious days and seasons with which students are familiar and which have meaning for them.
3. Various occasions of crisis for the students throughout the school year, such as: leaving home, making new friends, discouragement, etc.
4. Crises of thought which come as a result of the "expanding horizons" of a college education, such as: change in religious beliefs, general philosophy of life, social attitudes.
5. Occasions of general enthusiasm, such as interest in sports, or in an especially beautiful display of nature, as in spring.
6. Emphasis on the commonly accepted decencies and ethical code of the students and the acknowledged vices: pride, envy, intemperance, love of money, etc.
7. Birthdays of people whose lives will convey meaningful lessons to student groups.

A schedule of services showing how these themes may be worked out in a program of worship for chapel services follows. Following this schedule a calendar of events suggestive of themes for worship leaders is given. The remainder of the chapter is made up of twelve services of worship showing how these themes may be worked out in actual services, using the division of objectives and the standards for services previously explained. There are six services to illustrate the ethical purposes of worship and six (of four types) to illustrate the appreciational purposes of worship.

A SUGGESTED SCHEDULE OF SERVICES OF WORSHIP FOR EACH WEEK OF THE COLLEGE YEAR

SEPTEMBER
    1. A service of worship for the beginning of school
    2. A service of worship for students away from home
    3. A service of dedication to the purposes of the college

October

4. A service of worship in appreciation of friendship
5. A service of worship in praise of the beauties of autumn
6. A service of humility
7. A service in praise of the Christian grace of good cheer

November

8. A service of worship for true sportsmanship
9. A service of worship for international peace
10. A service of worship for social justice
11. A service of thanksgiving

December

12. A service of dedication to Jesus the Christ
13. A service of worship for Advent
14. A service of worship for Christmas

January

15. A service of worship for the beginning of a new year
16. A service of worship in appreciation of winter
17. A service of worship in praise of sincerity
18. A service of worship in devotion to racial brotherhood

February

1. A service of worship for the beginning of a new semester
2. A service of worship in appreciation of the life of Lincoln
3. A service of worship in praise of the Blessed Life
4. A service of dedication to a life of useful work

March

5. A service of worship for cleanness of life
6. A service of dedication to the religion of love
7. A service of worship for strength in meeting temptation
8. A service of repentance

April

9. A service of worship for Palm Sunday
10. A service of worship for Easter
11. A service of worship in praise of spring
12. A service of worship for help in resisting discouragement

May

13. A service for worshipers who may be changing beliefs
14. A service of worship for mother's day
15. A service for guidance in the use of possessions
16. A service of worship for Memorial Day

June

17. A service of the commandments
18. A service of worship for the close of school

CALENDAR OF EVENTS OF INTEREST TO THE LEADER OF COLLEGE WORSHIP

SEPTEMBER
    Labor Day
      6. Jane Addams born
    Beginning of school
    17. Constitution Day
    Jewish day of Atonement

OCTOBER
      4. St. Francis of Assisi born
      4. Jean François Millet born
      6. William Tyndale died
      7. James Whitcomb Riley born
    12. Columbus discovered America
    14. William Penn died
    20. Sir Christopher Wren born
    22. Franz Liszt born
    27. Theodore Roosevelt born
    29. John Keats born
    Football season
    Fraternity rushing
    Autumn

NOVEMBER
    Election day
    10. Martin Luther born
    11. Armistice Day
    13. Robert Louis Stevenson born
    14. Booker T. Washington died
    21. Mayflower Compact signed 1620
    Thanksgiving Day
    Advent Sunday

DECEMBER
    Advent
      7. John Milton born
    11. Emily Dickinson born
    13. Phillips Brooks born
    16. Beethoven born
    17. John Greenleaf Whittier born
    18. Edward MacDowell born
    25. Clara Barton born
    25. Christmas

JANUARY
      1. New Year's Day

6. Epiphany
  16. Prohibition went into effect 1920
  17. Benjamin Franklin born
  19. Robert E. Lee born
  19. Edgar Allen Poe born
  25. Robert Burns born
  27. Mozart born
  29. William McKinley born
  31. Schubert born
  31. Child Labor Day
  End of the first semester

FEBRUARY
  Beginning of the second semester
   3. Mendelssohn born
   3. Woodrow Wilson died 1924
   5. Roger Williams born
   7. Charles Dickens born
   8. John Ruskin born
  11. Thomas A. Edison born
  12. Abraham Lincoln born
  12. Charles Darwin born
  19. Copernicus born
  22. George Washington born
  22. James Russell Lowell born
  23. Johann Gutenberg died
  23. Handel born
  27. Henry Wadsworth Longfellow born
  Winter
  Basketball season
  Ash Wednesday

MARCH
  Lent
   4. Inaugural day (each four years)
  17. St. Patrick's Day
  19. David Livingstone born
  21. Johann Sebastian Bach born
  21. Spring
  26. Robert Frost born
  31. Haydn born
  Palm Sunday

APRIL
  Holy Week
  Good Firday

Easter
   3. Edward Everett Hale born
   7. William Wordsworth born
   10. William Booth born
   13. Thomas Jefferson born
   23. William Shakespeare born

MAY
   1. International Labor Day
   2. Leonardo da Vinci died
   4. Horace Mann born
   5. Arbor Day
   7. Johannes Brahms born
   Mothers Day—second Sunday
   12. Florence Nightingale born
   22. Richard Wagner born
   25. Ralph Waldo Emerson born
   31. Walt Whitman born

JUNE
   Commencement
   1. John Masefield born
   8. Robert Schumann born
   14. Flag Day
   14. Harriet Beecher Stowe born
   15. Edward Grieg born
   15. Magna Carta signed 1215
   17. Charles Gounod born
   22. Summer
   28. John Wesley born

JULY
   4. Independence Day
   4. Stephen Foster born
   6. John Huss born
   10. John Calvin born
   10. Whistler born
   14. Bastille Day
   16. Sir Joshua Reynolds born
   17. Isaac Watts born

AUGUST
   6. Alfred Tennyson born
   9. Adoniram Judson born
   28. Tolstoi born

B. Illustrative Services

1. Services with Ethical Purposes

A. A SERVICE OF WORSHIP IN DEVOTION TO RACIAL BROTHERHOOD

The Prelude
The Processional Hymn:
  (a) O Zion haste, 270 ASH *
  (b) Gather us in, thou Love, 261 ASH
The Scripture Lesson:
  (a) Luke 10: 29–37 Parable of the Good Samaritan *or*
  (b) A sermonic version of the Parable by Dr. Charles E. Jefferson:
   . . . A certain man went down from Jerusalem to Jericho and on his way fell among brigands who beat him and stripped off his clothes and left him bleeding and half dead. A preacher came along, on his way to conduct public services in Jerusalem. He was all dressed up, as a man must be who is going to conduct public worship. He looked at the man. He saw that he was bloody. Now, a preacher does not want to get blood on his cuffs, so this preacher hurried on. He arrived in Jerusalem, I presume, just in time to begin the service of worship. By and by another man came along. This man was a singer in the choir. He belonged to a vested choir. Now, if one is to sing in public worship he does not want to have his vestments soiled or in any way disarranged. This singer saw that the man was bloody and half dead and so he hurried on to Jerusalem in order to sing. But by and by an infidel came along. That was what a Samaritan was. He rejected two-thirds of the Bible, and refused to worship in Jerusalem. He was a renegade, an apostate, a reprobate, a dirty dog, in the opinion of every pious Jew. But this dirty dog got off his donkey, put his arms underneath the man who was bleeding and half dead, put him on his donkey, took him to a hotel, paid the hotel bill, and Jesus closes the story with the exhortation, "Now you go and do that too."
The Choral Response (if desired):
  Lord, have mercy, have mercy upon us (Kyrie Eleison). 531 HLA
The Litany of Thanksgiving
  Leader: America is a land of one people, gathered from many countries. Some have come for love of freedom and some have sought opportunity. Whatever the cause that drew them, each has brought his gift. Irish and Scotch, English and Dutch, Italian, Greek and French, Negro, Spaniard, Slav, Norse and Teuton—all have come bearing gifts and have laid them on the Altar of America.

* In this section the following abbreviations are used: ASH—*American Student Hymnal;* HLA—*Hymns for the Living Age;* NHAY—*The New Hymnal for American Youth;* MH—*The Methodist Hymnal.*

Response: For all these gifts we thank Thee, Lord.
Leader: Some have brought their music.
Response: For all these gifts we thank Thee, Lord.
Leader: Some have brought their poetry.
Response: For all these gifts we thank Thee, Lord.
Leader: Some have brought their art.
Response: For all these gifts we thank Thee, Lord.
Leader: Then each, too, has brought some homely thing, some touch of the familiar field or forest—a favorite tree or fruit, a flower from a well-remembered garden. And all brought hands with which to work; and all brought minds that could conceive both truth and beauty; and all brought hearts filled high with hope, stout hearts to drive live minds, live minds to guide strong hands.
Response: For all these gifts we thank Thee, Lord. (1) [28]

The Prayer of Resolution (unison or by leader):
Dear God
Since time immemorial
There have been race prejudices:
And since time immemorial
We have heeded the dictates of ugly conventions;
And we, the Youth of the world,
Have been in the background,
And now
We want to come forward
And think for ourselves,
And rule our own lives;
And we feel
That the happiness of the world
Rests on the shoulders of Youth.
It's up to us to sweep aside all race prejudices
And to break down barriers everywhere
Between color, race, and creed;
And it's up to us to say,
"There shall be no more war."
Dear God
We believe this, our greatest fault
Is race prejudice,
For it holds more baseness and cruelty
Than any other fault
In the wide world. . . .
Dear God,

---

[28] The numbers in parentheses at the ends of the selections indicate the sources from which the material was taken. See SOURCES, p. 118, this study.

Help us to overcome these, our faults,
Help us to forget our international suspicions,
Our animosities and hates.
Help us, the Youth of the world,
To bring all nations together in peace;
Help us to meet the world in peace;
Help us to meet the world as brothers;
Help us to walk joyously in the open sunshine of world friendship. (2)
    (Instead of this prayer, the "Litany of Repentance" on page 91 of *Fellowship Prayers* could be used.)
The Choral Response (or a hymn):
  (a) Let your light so shine, 400 ASH
  (b) O Blessed Son of God, 255 ASH (stanza five)
The Prayer of Dedication (unison):
    O God, our Father, we dedicate ourselves anew to thee and thy service. Put into the heart of each one of us such a love that we may truly love our neighbors as ourselves, a love that leaps the boundaries of race, or color, or creed, or kind; that knows no distinction of class; that reaches out a saving hand even unto the least of these, our brethren. . . . Amen.   (3)
The Address (if desired)
The Hymn:
  (a) At length there dawns the glorious day, 256 ASH
  (b) In Christ there is no East or West, 273 ASH
  (c) The crest and crowning of all good, 259 ASH
The Benediction:
For all the oppressed afar off who sigh for liberty;
For all lovers of the people who strive to break their shackles;
For all who dare to believe in the divine democracy of thy kingdom:
Bless thou our nation and all who dwell therein now and henceforth.
Amen.   (4)

B. A SERVICE OF WORSHIP FOR INTERNATIONAL PEACE

An Armistice Day Service

A Prelude of Reverence and Power
The Processional Hymn:
  (a) God the Omnipotent! 264 ASH, 284 NHAY
  (b) America triumphant! 280 ASH
The Invocation:
    O Lord, our God, Our hearts are filled with gratitude in memory of thy great goodness. Thou makest wars to cease unto the end of the earth; thou burnest the chariots with fire. May righteousness and justice be established in all the earth, and thus may the time soon come

when nation shall not lift up sword against nation, neither shall they learn war any more. In the name of thy Son, the Prince of Peace, we ask it. Amen. (5)

The Gloria in Excelsis (395 ASH; use stanzas 1 and 2 or all; or use the Doxology instead of the Gloria.)

The Confession:

Victor Hugo looked to our day with great hope. He wrote: "In the Twentieth Century war will be dead, the scaffold will be dead, frontier boundaries will be dead, dogmas will be dead; man will live. He will possess something higher than all these—a great country, the whole earth, and a great hope, the whole heaven." How disappointed Victor Hugo would be! For this longed-for Twentieth Century brought to history the most terrible conflict of all time. Today we celebrate the anniversary of the end of that war, and—we hope—the end of all wars. Let us hear the indictment which Thomas Carlyle brought against war as a means of settling international disputes.

The Reading:

What, speaking in quite unofficial language, is the net purpose and upshot of war? To my own knowledge, for example, there dwell and toil, in the British village of Dumdrudge, usually some five hundred souls. From these, by certain "Natural Enemies" of the French, there are successfully selected, during the French war, say thirty able-bodied men; Dumdrudge, at her own expense, has suckled and nursed them: she has, not without difficulty and sorrow, fed them up to manhood, and even trained them to crafts, so that one can weave, another build, another hammer, and the weakest can stand under thirty stone avoirdupois. Nevertheless, amid much weeping and swearing, they are selected; all dressed in red, and shipped away, at the public charges, some two thousand miles, or say, only, to the south of Spain, and fed there till wanted. And now to that same spot, in the south of Spain, are thirty similar French artisans, from a French Dumdrudge, in like manner wending; till at length, after infinite effort, the two parties come into actual juxtaposition, and Thirty stands fronting Thirty, each with a gun in his hand. Straightway the word "Fire" given and they blow the souls out of one another, and in place of sixty brisk useful craftsmen, the world has sixty dead carcasses, which it must bury, and anew shed tears for. Had these men any quarrel? Busy as the Devil is, not the smallest! They lived far enough apart; were the entirest strangers; nay, in so wide a Universe, there was even, unconsciously, by Commerce, some mutual helpfulness between them. How then? Simpleton! their Governors had fallen out; and, instead of shooting one another, had the cunning to make these poor blockheads shoot.

The Treaty for the Renunciation of War (leader reading):

Led by the desire of the peoples of the earth for continued peace, nearly all the nations of the world, including the United States of America, have sworn in solemn treaty to renounce war as an instrument of national policy. Hear the articles of the treaty (audience stands):

ARTICLE I

The high contracting parties solemnly declare in the names of their respective peoples that they condemn recourse to war for the solution of international controversies, and renounce it as an instrument of national policy in their relations with one another.

ARTICLE II

The high contracting parties agree that the settlement or solution of all disputes or conflicts, of whatever nature or of whatever origin they may be, which may arise among them, shall never be sought except by pacific means.

The Pledge of the People (audience standing and saying):

We, the people here assembled, offer praise to Almighty God that his spirit has with such grace and power moved upon the nations. As we have in times past offered our lives and treasure to the fortunes of war, so now, at the threshold of a new dispensation, with war outlawed, we dedicate ourselves and our mighty nation to the fortunes of peace through justice.

The Prayer (leader or in unison):
Eternal God, Father of all souls,
Grant unto us such clear vision of the sin of war
That we may earnestly seek that coöperation between nations
Which alone can make war impossible.
As man by his inventions has made the whole world
Into one neighborhood,
Grant that he may, by his coöperation, make the whole world
Into one brotherhood.
Help us to break down all race prejudice.
Stay the greed of those who profit by war, and
The ambitions of those who seek an imperialistic conquest
Drenched in blood.
Guide all statesmen to seek a just basis
For international action in the interests of peace.
Arouse in the whole body of the people an adventurous willingness
As they sacrificed greatly for war,
So, also, for international good-will;
So dare bravely, think wisely, decide resolutely,
As to achieve triumphantly. Amen. (6)

The Address (if desired)

The Recessional Hymn:
  (a) Not in vain the distance beacons, 265 ASH
  (b) In Christ there is no East or West, 273 ASH
The Benediction: Now the Lord of peace himself give us peace at all times in all ways. The Lord be with us all. (I Thess. 3:16)
The Postlude

C. A SERVICE OF WORSHIP FOR SOCIAL JUSTICE

The Prelude
The Hymn:
  (a) Where Cross the crowded ways of life, 60 ASH
  (b) Lord, speak to me that I may speak, 216 ASH
  (c) My Master was so very poor, 110 NHAY
The Call to Worship (leader):

O Thou great teacher of men, with whom are hid all the treasures of wisdom and knowledge, look down upon us, we beseech thee, a company of students who are trying to feel our way a little farther into the mystery of thy world. Open our minds to every new insight; make our spirits sensitive to every fresh impression. Suffer us not to lose the whole in the parts—to sacrifice the distant for the near; but speaking truth in love, may we grow in all things unto him whom thou hast given us for our model, the Christ who is the way and the truth and the life. Amen. (7)

The Choral Response (if desired):
  (a) Father Almighty, bless us, 44 ASH, second stanza only, *or*
  (b) Let the words of my mouth, 338 NHAY
The Scripture Reading: James 1:27–2:20
The Problem (Hamlin Garland):

>   What shall I do to be just?
>   What shall I do for the gain
>   Of the world—for its sadness?
>   Teach me, O Seers that I trust!
>   Chart me the difficult main
>   Leading me out of my sorrow and madness;
>   Preach me out of the purging of pain.
>
>   Shall I wrench from my finger the ring
>   To cast to the tramp at my door?
>   Shall I tear off each luminous thing
>   To drop in the palm of the poor?
>   What shall I do to be just?
>   Teach me, O Ye in the light,
>   Whom the poor and the rich alike trust:
>   My heart is aflame to be right. (8)

The Condition:
>   Always the poor are with us,
>   Age-long is their tread.
>   Anxious or sodden their faces,
>   Weary and bent their forms,
>   Heavy, heavy their footsteps,
>   Shuffling over the earth.
>   When wild nights are shrieking
>   And the nights are black,
>   Do you not hear them shuffling,
>   Shuffling beneath your window,
>   Shuffling past your door?
>   Millions upon millions,
>   Poor, tired, patient feet,
>   Shuffling, shuffling, shuffling,
>   Can you not hear the shuffling,
>   Heavy tread of the poor?   (9)

The Prayer of Sympathy and Dedication:
  God of love,
  We pray thee this day for the poor and outcast of this land:
  For those who from year's end to year's end
  Have never enough for their body's need:
  For those who live perpetually on the bitter edge of starvation:
  For those whose lot is continually shame and oppression,
  Who for no fault of their own are loathed and spat upon:
  For those who labor incessantly,
  In heat and thirst, for a miserable reward:
  For those who are driven through want to shame and sin:
  For those who have no hope in this life or beyond:
  For those who labor helplessly for cruel masters:
  For those who are bound fast by dark superstition and horrible dread:
  For those who lack bitterly thy light and thy life:—
  For all these, O our Father, we beseech thy grace.

  And we ask thee for a share of thy spirit,
  That we may give ourselves, gladly and generously,
  In the constant endeavour to rescue and to emancipate
  These, the needy and helpless ones of our nation—
  These without whom she cannot be saved.   (10)

The Address (if desired)
The Hymn:
  (a) The voice of God is calling, 235 ASH
  (b) I thank thee, Lord, for strength of arm, 211 ASH
  (c) Heaven is here, where hymns of gladness, 221 ASH

The Benediction:
> O Most Merciful, whose love to us is mighty, long-suffering, and infinitely tender, enable us to carry out from this place the peace and strength that here we have gained. Because we have walked here awhile with Thee, may we be able to walk more patiently with man. Send us forth with love to the fallen, hope for the despairing, strength to impart to the weak and wayward; and carry on through us the work Thou didst commence in thy Son our Brother Man and Saviour God. Amen. (11)

D. A SERVICE OF WORSHIP IN PREPARATION FOR CHRISTMAS

A Prelude of Great Joy

The Call to Worship:
> O loving Father, who hast brought us again to the glad season when we commemorate the birth of thy Son, Jesus of Nazareth, grant that his spirit may be born anew in our hearts this day and that we may joyfully welcome him to reign over us. Open our ears that we may hear again the angelic chorus of old; open our lips that we too may sing with uplifted hearts, Glory to God in the highest, and on earth peace, good will toward men. Amen. (12)

The Hymn:
  (a) It swells upon the noon-day breeze, 250 ASH
  (b) Hills of the north, rejoice, 267 ASH
  (c) The kings of the East are riding, 92 NHAY

The Psalm of Praise: Psalm 98

The Gloria Patri

The Christmas Litany:
> Leader: God, tabernacled among men;
> People: Have mercy upon us.
> L.: Let us give thanks:
>   That at this Christmastide the world is listening to the song of peace.
> P.: We praise thee, O God, and bless thy Holy Name.
> L.: That men of good will everywhere are opening a door to peace;
> P.: We praise thee, O God, and bless thy Holy Name.
> L.: O Immanuel our King and Lawgiver, the Desire of all nations and their Saviour,
> P.: Come and save us, O Lord our God.
> L.: From turning away from the inn of our hearts the Christ that is to be;
> P.: Good Lord, deliver us.
> L.: From hardening our hearts against the angelic message;
> P.: Good Lord, deliver us.
> L.: That we may be the people of good will, building nations of good will;
> P.: We beseech thee to hear us, good Lord.

L.: That we may make room in our national life for the dwelling of the world's Redeemer;
P.: We beseech thee to hear us, good Lord.
L.: That the rulers of the earth may worship at the Manger where love is revealed in weakness;
P.: We beseech thee to hear us, good Lord.
L.: That all who profess and call themselves Christians may reveal to others, God manifest in man;
P.: We beseech thee to hear us, good Lord.
L.: That in the power of all Incarnation, Christendom may shape its common life to the law of love;
P.: We beseech thee to hear us, good Lord.
L.: That all peoples may learn that only by emptying themselves of glory can they be filled with the spirit of God;
P.: We beseech thee to hear us, good Lord. (13)

The Collect (leader and people):
Our Father, who from the foundation of the ages hast prepared for our present and eternal happiness, grant us wisdom and willingness to make preparations to receive Thine unspeakable Gift. As the spirit of the Yuletide has taken possession of the workshop and market place, to supply the Christmas of a thousand packages, of hurried and worried people, so may the vital and unseen influences of the silent night, and the angel song, and the Christ-child claim us. May the Christmas of the ceaseless spirit of love, peace, and good-will wholly possess us, to the honor and glory of Christ, who comes to reign in our hearts. In His Name. Amen. (14)

The Address (if desired)

The Hymn:
(a) Hail to the Lord's Anointed, 244 ASH, 301 NHAY
(b) O come, O come, Immanuel, 75 NHAY

The Benediction:
Almighty God, who in thy Providence hast made all ages a preparation for the kingdom of thy Son; we beseech thee to make ready our hearts for the brightness of thy glory and the fullness of thy blessing in Jesus Christ our Lord. Amen. (15)

The Postlude

E. A SERVICE OF WORSHIP FOR CHRISTMAS

A Christmas Prelude

The Call to Worship:
Everywhere, everywhere, Christmas tonight!
Christmas in lands of the fir-tree and pine,
Christmas in lands of the palm-tree and vine,
Christmas where snow peaks stand solemn and white,

Christmas where cornfields stand sunny and bright.
Christmas where children are hopeful and gay,
Christmas where old men are patient and gray,
Christmas where peace, like a dove in his flight,
Broods o'er brave men in the thick of the fight;
Everywhere, everywhere, Christmas tonight!   (16)

The Hymn:
  (a) Hark, the herald angels sing,   360 ASH   *or*
  (b) O come, all ye faithful,   298 ASH   *or*
  (c) There's a song in the air,   84 NHAY

The Christmas Story:
  (a) St. Luke 2: 4–20 *or*
  (b) "Bethlehem" by Bliss Carman

> Long was the road to Bethlehem,
> Where Joseph and his Mary came.
> They are travel-worn, the day grows late,
> As they reach the town with its towered gate—
> The city of David's royal line—
> And the stars of eve are beginning to shine.
> They must seek a place where the poor may rest,
> For Mary is weary and overpressed.
>   And it is the sixth hour.
>
> They come to an inn and knock on the door,
> Asking a little space—no more
> Than a humble shelter in their need.
> The innkeeper gives them scanty heed.
> Little for strangers does he care—
> His house is full. They must seek elsewhere.
> Fearing to find no place that day,
> Heavy at heart they turn away.
>   And it is the seventh hour.
>
> In weariness and sore perplexed,
> To a larger house they venture next.
> Joseph for pity's sake begs again
> A lodging for Mary in her pain.
> They are poor Galileans, plain to be told—
> Their garments are worn, their sandals are old.
> The fat innkeeper jingles his keys,
> And refuses shelter to such as these.
>   And it is the ninth hour.
>
> Where now they turn the woman is kind,
> Tho the place is crowded, still she would find

Room for them somehow—moved at the sight
Of this gentle girl in her urgent plight,
Who tells of her hope and her strength far spent,
And seems to her woman's heart God-sent.
But the surly landlord roars in wrath
And send them forth on their lonely path.
    And it is the eleventh hour.

Still seeking a place to lay them down,
They come at length, on the edge of the town,
To a cattle-shed with sagging door,
Thankful for only the stable floor,
When an old gray donkey crowds to the wall
To make them room in his straw-laid stall,
And the cattle low at the stifled wail
Of a woman's voice in sore travail.
    It is midnight and Mary's hour.

Over the place a great new star
Sheds glory and wonder beheld afar,
While all through the height of heaven there flies
The word of a seraph voice that cries,
"Glory to God, this wondrous morn
On earth the Saviour Christ is born."

The Anthem *or* a hymn of praise:
  (a) Christmas anthem as selected
  (b) It came upon the midnight clear,   245 ASH, 78 NHAY
  (c) The first Noel,   328 ASH, 79 NHAY

The Prayer:

    Almighty God, our heavenly Father, in whose grace all our light is born, and in whose love is the fountain of our festivity, mercifully lead us into the holy secret of Christmas-tide. Take us into the innermost room of its holy joy. Forbid that we should remain in the outer courts, dwelling amid its merely carnal pleasures, satisfied with the merriment that dies with the day, and contented with the happiness that passes with the fading flower and with the withering leaf. Bring us, our Father, into the eternal things of this blessed season. Bring us into the things that abide, into the love that manifests itself in unfailing good-will, into the joy that rings Christmas bells all the year round. Teach us, our Father, the full meaning of Jesus' birth. Make our hearts to glow with gladness in the great redemption Christ brings us, and with adoring love to him, to thee, to the indwelling Spirit, and to all humankind. From this day let our souls be so fed on Christ that we shall generate the fragrance of his loving-kindness wherever we walk. From this hour let infancy, childhood, helplessness, poverty, and all human need appeal to us with compelling power and draw us into ceaseless and effective service in the name of our Saviour. (J. H. Jowett.)

And Grant, O Lord, that we may so enjoy our holiday at this season, that our bodies may be strengthened, our minds renewed, and our energies quickened for the perfect freedom of thy service; through Jesus Christ our Lord. Amen. (17)

The Prayer Response (if desired; by quartet or choir):
  (a) Lord Jesus, Son of Mary, 86 NHAY (first stanza) *or*
  (b) Silent night, holy night, 302 ASH (third stanza)

The Christmas Dedication (standing; recited in unison or by leader):
  In the spirit of Christmas we unite in hearty good will to all mankind . . . Forswearing all enmities and the distinctions that divide, we commit ourselves to the building up of Peace on Earth and Good Will among men. (18)

The Hymn:
  (a) Christians, lo, the star appeareth, 220 ASH *or*
  (b) O Little town of Bethlehem, 330 ASH

The Benediction:
> "Glory to God!" the sounding skies
> Loud with their anthems ring;
> "Peace to the earth, good-will to men,
> From heaven's eternal King!"   Amen.

The Christmas Postlude

F. A SERVICE OF WORSHIP IN PRAISE OF SINCERITY

The Prelude

The Hymn:
  (a) The Lord is my shepherd, 365 ASH
  (b) Guide me, O Thou great Jehovah, 366 ASH

The Call to Worship:
  Who shall ascend into the hill of the Lord? or who shall stand in his holy place? He that hath clean hands and a pure heart; who hath not lifted up his soul unto vanity, nor sworn deceitfully. He shall receive the blessing of the Lord, and righteousness from the God of his salvation.

  Centuries ago Homer wrote, "Hateful to me as are the gates of Hell, is he who, hiding one thing in his heart, utters another." And Socrates is quoted as saying, "The shortest and surest way to live with Honour in the world, is to be in reality what we would appear to be." No less in our day do men despise the lack of sincerity. Yet we know that absolute sincerity is not always easily achieved. But hear what Jesus had to say to men whose sincerity he suspected.

The Scripture Lesson: Mt. 23: 23–28. The inside of the cup.

The Poem—"Sermons We See":
   I'd rather see a sermon than hear one any day;
   I'd rather one should walk with me than merely tell the way.
   The eye's a better pupil and more willing than the ear,
   Fine counsel is confusing, but example's always clear;
   And the best of all the preachers are the men who live their creeds.
   I soon can learn to do it if you'll let me see it done;
   I can watch your hands in action, but your tongue too fast may run.
   And the lecture you deliver may be very wise and true,
   But I'd rather get my lessons by observing what you do;
   For I might misunderstand you and the high advice you give,
   But there's no misunderstanding how you act and how you live. (19)
The Prayer:
   Divine Leader, we want always to ring true. May we not be hypocrites, boasting of our goodness or posing for credit which we do not deserve. May we never deceive or cheat people in any way. Make us four-square to the right, always true to ourselves and others.
   Sometimes we want to be showy like glittering tinsel, or boastful like shiny brass; but our better selves speak to us and say, "Be pure gold, for the world will see through and know you for what you are." It is hard to follow this inner voice when we see so much counterfeit being accepted in the world. Oh, keep us from trying to gain through make-believe, and help us to build, day by day, those genuine qualities which will make us strong Christians. Give us power to be our true selves all the time. Amen. (20)
The Hymn: I would be true, 180 ASH
The Benediction:
   May we to our own selves be true, and may it follow, as the night the day, that we shall not then be false to any man. In this determination may we have the blessing and the guidance of our heavenly Father. Amen.

2. Services of Appreciation: Nature

G. A SERVICE IN PRAISE OF THE BEAUTIES OF AUTUMN

A Prelude of Beauty
A Processional Hymn:
   (a) Let the whole creation cry, 45 ASH, 44 NHAY *or*
   (b) The heavens declare thy glory, 50 ASH, 41 NHAY
An Exclamation of joy: (Read by leader or special reader)
            O world, I can not hold thee close enough!
               Thy woods, thy wide gray skies!
               Thy mists that roll and rise!
            Thy woods, this autumn day, that ache and sag

> And all but cry with color! That gaunt crag
> To crush! To lift the lean of that black bluff!
> World, world, I can not get thee close enough!
>
> Long have I known a glory in it all
>   But never knew I this;
>   Here such a passion is
> As stretcheth me apart—Lord, I do fear
> Thou'st made the world too beautiful this year;
> My soul is all but out of me—let fall
> No burning leaf; prithee, let no bird call. (21)

The Scriptures: Psalm 148: 1–6 (read in unison or by reader)

A Confession. (First reader reads):

> A curve in the road and a hillside
> Clear cut against the sky;
> A tall tree tossed by autumn wind,
> And a white cloud riding high;
> Ten men went along that road;
> And all but one passed by,
> He saw the hill and the tree and the cloud
> With an artist's mind and eye;
> And he put them down on canvas—
> For the other nine men to buy. (22)

(Second reader reads):

> The World is too much with us; late and soon
> Getting and spending, we lay waste our powers;
> Little we see in Nature that is ours;
> We have given our hearts away, a sordid boon!
>
> This sea that bares her bosom to the moon,
> The winds that will be howling at all hours,
> Are up-gathered now like sleeping flowers,
> For this, for everything, we are out of tune;
> It moves us not.—Great God! I'd rather be
> A Pagan, suckled in a creed outworn,—
> So might I, standing on this pleasant lea,
> Have glimpses that would make me less forlorn;
> Have sight of Proteus rising from the sea;
> Or hear old Triton blow his wreathéd horn. (23)

A Prayer of Appreciation (unison or by leader):

We thank thee, Lord, for the tapestry of a hundred hues on the hillsides of Fall these days. We thank Thee, that as we ride along the country ways we find Thy reds, and golds, and yellows, and browns, and purple patches splashed everywhere. We thank Thee that the hillsides of Fall are like rich Oriental tapestries. We thank Thee for the crimson beauty and

> "The glory that the wood receives
> At sunset in its brazen leaves."

But most of all . . . we thank Thee, Lord, that thou hast put color into our lives. There is nothing dull and dead in our lives since Thou hast come into our hearts. Thou hast painted life as rich as a Fall hillside. Thou has filled our hearts with light and laughter and love. Thou has come, and since Thou hast come, Life is beautiful with color. Amen. (24)

An Address (if desired)

A Recessional Hymn:
  (a) My God I thank thee who hast made *or*
      204 ASH, 51 NHAY
  (b) The heavens declare thy glory
      50 ASH, 39 NHAY

The Benediction:
  May God bless us with a loving sense of His near presence, to guide us, to protect us, and to help us; may we all know what it is to walk close with Him all our life long. Amen.

H. A SERVICE OF WORSHIP IN APPRECIATION OF WINTER

The Prelude of Beauty

The Call to Worship (leader or in unison):
  (a) Psalm 97 *or*
  (b) The One Thousandth Psalm:
    O God, we thank thee for everything:
    For the glory and beauty and wonder of the world,
    For the glory of springtime, the tints of the flowers and their fragrance;
    For the glory of the summer flowers, the roses and cardinals and clethra;
    For the glory of the autumn, the scarlet and crimson and gold of the forest;
    For the glory of winter, the pure snow on the shrubs and trees.
    We thank thee that thou hast placed us here
    To use thy gifts for the good of all. (25)

The Hymn:
  (a) All beautiful the march of days, 48 ASH *or*
  (b) God of the earth, the sky, the sea, 55 ASH

The Confession (reader or responsively; may be omitted):
> What is this life if, full of care,
> We have no time to stand and stare.

No time to stand beneath the boughs
And stare as long as sheep or cows.

No time to see, when woods we pass,
Where squirrels hide their nuts in grass.

No time to see, in broad daylight,
Streams full of stars, like stars at night.

No time to turn at Beauty's glance,
And watch her feet, how they can dance.

No time to wait till her mouth can
Enrich that smile her eyes began.

A poor life this, if, full of care,
We have no time to stand and stare.   (26)

The Reading of the Divine Law (reader):

Nature never did betray
The heart that loved her; 'tis her privilege,
Through all the years of this our life, to lead
From joy to joy, for she can so inform
The mind that is within us, so impress
With quietness and beauty, and so feed
With lofty judgments, that neither evil tongues,
Rash judgments, nor the sneers of selfish men,
Nor greetings where no kindness is, nor all
The dreary intercourse of daily life,
Shall e'er prevail against us, or disturb
Our cheerful faith, that all which we behold
Is full of blessings.   (27)

The Prayer of Appreciation: (Choose prayer a or b according to the weather.)

(a) For a snowy day:

Dear God, the snow has covered every field and fence, and tree and trail, and heart and home, and love and life this Winter's . . . morning. Thy world is beautiful to us this day.

Every tree is a Christmas tree, although Christmas has long since passed us by. It is snowy, blustery March, but the world is full of glorious Christmas trees this morning. Every branch and limb is immaculate with beauty. We awoke to a Fairyland this day, Thy Fairyland of love and light.

The muddy roads and the dead and desolate winter fields are cured of all their ills this morning. Thy snow has hidden every scar and every ugly spot on all the earth.

Like the tides that sweep in from the sea to cover every ugly mudhole and to fill every crevice, so thy tides of snow have come during the night to hide every ugly spot and to cover every scar on the earth.

So may Thy love to us this day make us immaculate. So may Thy love crown every life with light, and make every heart a happy Christmas tree. So may Thy love cover every scar in our poor, lonely, devastated lives.

It is dark and gloomy this day overhead, and the clouds are gray with desolation, but it is beautiful on the earth. The white snow is a symbol of Thy white life and Thy white Christ; Thy white promises and Thy white cross. Thou has not forgotten us, dear Lord, and Thou hast made our world beautiful today.

And we thank Thee for that! Amen. (28)

(b) For a snowless day:

When Winter came we thought Thee gone forever from us, dear God of our needs!

We looked upon the earth and it was bare. We looked to the trees and they were leafless, save for a scattered leaf here and there, lonely as a lone bird in a Winter sky. We looked for flowers, and there were none anywhere, for they had all died. We looked for violets and buttercups, and the earth could offer us naught but memories and sighs.

Dear God, it's a lonely world in Winter time. The trees are so bare, and the fields are so cheerless, and the river is so naked. Art Thou gone forever? Wilt Thou never come back to us? Hast Thou forgotten us entirely?

And the answer comes across the Winter fields from Thee; across the lonely ice-bound rivers; across the dead fields; across the empty nests of birds: "Remember the Resurrection Time! The seeds will burst again after a while, and violets will dot the land and dandelions will scatter star-dust everywhere again; and grass will grow. I am not gone. I have not forgotten thee. I am at work getting ready for the Resurrection of Spring. I love thee still!"

That is Thy word, dear Lord, these barren days, and that word heartens our souls and we smile again, and we take new lease on life, and we leap with laughter in our souls and shout the glad news to all humanity that thou dost still love us like a Father and that thou art just away preparing the surprise of Spring for us; preparing the glorious event of the Resurrection. Amen! Amen! Amen! (29)

The Hymn:
(a) The gray hills taught me patience, 161 ASH *or*
(b) He who himself and God would know, 56 ASH

The Benediction:
The Lord bless us and keep us;
The Lord make His face to shine upon us, and be gracious unto us.

The Lord lift up His countenance upon us, and give us peace, both now and forevermore. Amen.

Services of Appreciation: Personal Problems

I. A SERVICE OF WORSHIP FOR TRUE SPORTSMANSHIP

A Prelude of Vigorous Dignity

A Hymn:
  (a) God of our boyhood (youth), 179 ASH, 162 NHAY *or*
  (b) Fight the good fight with all thy might, 158 ASH, 207 NHAY

The Scriptures: I Cor. 9: 24–27

A Prayer of a Sportsman:
> Dear Lord, in the battle that goes on through life
>   I ask but a field that is fair,
> A chance that is equal to all in the strife,
>   A courage to strive and to dare;
> And if I should win, let it be by the code
>   With my faith and my honor held high;
> And if I should lose, let me stand by the road,
>   And cheer as the winners go by.
>
> And Lord, may my shouts be ungrudging and clear
>   A tribute that comes from the heart,
> And let me not cherish a snarl or a sneer
>   Or play any sniveling part;
> Let me say, "There they ride, on whom laurel's bestowed
>   Since they played the game better than I."
> Let me stand with a smile by the side of the road,
>   And cheer as the winners go by.
>
> So grant me to conquer, if conquer I can,
>   By proving my worth in the fray,
> But teach me to lose like a regular man,
>   And not like a craven, I pray;
> Let me take off my hat to the warriors who strode
>   To victory splendid and high,
> Yea, teach me to stand by the side of the road
>   And cheer as the winners go by.   (30)

The Chorus or Choir:
  (a) Carry on—Service, 160 ASH *or*
  (b) The river of death—Newbolt, 159 ASH

A Prayer (in unison):
  When the game is going against me and there seems little chance to win, when there is a whole half to be played and I am hot and tired and sick at heart, then I pray, Divine Comrade, for strength to play the

game! It is easy enough to play when I am winning, when I feel fresh and there are no odds against me; but when things are going wrong and I am tempted to cheat, to grumble or to quit, then I need thy help.

I want to take life as a game and play it fair and hard. To do this I need some strong leader, so I pray that thou wilt always be with me. When I am a coward or tired or baffled, give me the sense that thou art by my side, telling me how to plan my way and giving me the courage to keep on. Be with me in the contest of to-day and all through life's course. Amen. (31)

An Address (if desired)

A Hymn:
  (a) We are not here to play, 185 ASH *or*
  (b) Awake, my soul, stretch every nerve, 165 ASH, 195 NHAY

The Benediction:
  May the love of God unite us; the joy of God inspire us; the peace of God enfold us; the courage of God sustain us; and the blessing of God, the Father, Son, and Holy Spirit, rest upon us forevermore. Amen.

J. A SERVICE OF WORSHIP FOR NEW YEAR'S

The Prelude

The Hymn:
  (a) O God, our help in ages past, 30 ASH *or*
  (b) Ring out, wild bells, to the wild sky, 324 ASH, 327 NHAY

The Call to Worship (leader):
  The tugging ship is unmoored; her sails are filling with the breeze; she sniffs the spray in her nostrils; her rigging grows taut like giant muscles; the course is set; the pilot is at the helm—the New Year is outward bound!
  We, too, are a ship.
  Each New Year we sail forth upon a sea heretofore untraveled by our humankind.
  The waves of ambition fill our sails, and the waves of adversity dash upon our decks.
  We touch at ports of call—the old familiar duties; but, O, the new ports with wealth of experience and color and adventure.
  Sail out, O soul of mine!
  That which alone matters is that the pilot has enough faith to trust the unknown! (32)

The Choral Response (choir or congregation):
  (a) Another year is dawning, 106 HLA, 571 MH *or*
  (b) O praise ye the Lord, 391 ASH *or*
  (c) The Doxology

The Confession (leader and people):

Ever-living God, by whose mercy we have come to the gateway of another year; grant that we may enter it with humble and grateful hearts; and confirm our resolution, we beseech thee, to walk more closely in thy way, and labor more faithfully in thy service, according to the teaching and example of thy Son our Lord. Let not the errors and offenses of the past cling to us, but pardon us and set us free, that with a purer purpose and a better hope, we may renew our vows in thy presence, and set forth under the guidance of thy Spirit to travel in that path which shineth more and more unto the perfect day of thy heavenly kingdom. Amen. (33)

The Scripture Reading: Mt. 25: 14–30. The Talents.

The Dedication:

Leader: To the development of richer and stronger inner lives for us all,
Response: We dedicate ourselves, O Lord.
L.: To those habits of health and exercise that build strong bodies, fit to be temples of thy Holy Spirit,
R.: We dedicate ourselves, O Lord.
L.: To the sacred tasks of mental enrichment that through books and study and honest thinking make our minds alert,
R.: We dedicate ourselves, O Lord.
L.: To the joys of social fellowship that make us indeed members one of another,
R.: We dedicate ourselves, O Lord.
L.: To the happy privilege of learning thy will, and of helping to achieve it in the world,
R.: We dedicate ourselves, O Lord. (34)

The Choral Response (if desired):

(a) Our Father, God, whose mercies still abide, 397 ASH *or*

(b) Father, let me dedicate all this year to thee, (first stanza) 105 HLA

The Address (if desired)

The Hymn:

(a) The Lord is my shepherd, 365 ASH, 57 NHAY *or*

(b) All the past we leave behind, 164 ASH, 211 NHAY

The Benediction:

Direct us, O Lord, in all our doings, with thy most gracious favor, and further us with thy continual help; that in all our works begun, continued, and ended in Thee, may we glorify Thy holy name, and finally, by thy mercy, obtain everlasting life, through Jesus Christ our Lord. Amen.

Services of Appreciation: Other People

K. A SERVICE IN APPRECIATION OF FRIENDSHIP

A Prelude of Reverent Music

A Hymn:

(a) O Master, let me walk with Thee, 214 ASH, 197 NHAY *or*
(b) Holy, holy, holy Lord, thy disciples, 75 ASH, 107 NHAY

The Call to Worship (leader):

Beloved, let us love one another: for love is of God; and every one that loveth is born of God, and knoweth God. He that loveth not knoweth not God; for God is love.

Forsooth, brother, fellowship is heaven, and the lack of fellowship is hell; fellowship is life and the lack of fellowship is death; and the deeds that ye do upon the earth, it is for fellowship's sake that ye do them. Therefore, I bid you not dwell in hell, but in heaven—upon earth, which is a part of heaven and forsooth no foul part. (35)

A Bidding Prayer:

Let us pray that God will give us sensitive hearts that we may be aware of the precious gift of human friendship.

(Here followeth a period of silent prayer.)

Let us give thanks for forgiveness which knows no measure, and for that quality of mind and heart which remembers no more our iniquity. . . .

(Here followeth a period of silent prayer.)

Let us bless God for courage we have received through the heroism of those who have rescued us from danger and temptation. . . .

(Here followeth a period of silent prayer.)

Let us pray that by the compassion given unto us we also shall be able to aid others in days of overwhelming need.

(Here followeth a period of silent prayer.)

Let us give thanks for the insight and the understanding of friends who have loved us when we have been unlovely, and have created within us by their trust, new hopes, new courage, and new purpose.

(Here followeth a period of silent prayer.)

Let us praise God for the faith of men and women whose steadfastness in adversity has often reëstablished our own belief.

(Here followeth a period of silent prayer.)

Let us give thanks for love which suffereth long and is kind, which hopeth all things, believeth all things and never faileth.

(Here followeth a period of silent prayer.)

Above all, let us give thanks for Jesus Christ, for His gentleness with little children, [and] for His friendship to young men and maidens. (36)

(Here followeth a period of silent prayer, ended, if desired, with a stanza of "O Love that will not let me go" sung by quartet, choir, or congregation.)

A Poem, "The Obligation of Friendship." (Read by leader or other reader):

    You ought to be fine for the sake of the folks
      Who think you are fine.

If others have faith in you doubly you're bound
  To stick to the line.
It's not only on you that dishonor descends:
You can't hurt yourself without hurting your friends.

You ought to be true for the sake of the folks
  Who believe you are true.
You never should stoop to a deed that your friends
  Think you wouldn't do.
If you're false to yourself, be the blemish but small,
You have injured your friends; you've been false to them all.

For friendship, my boy, is a bond between men
  That is founded on truth:
It believes in the best of the ones that it loves,
  Whether old man or youth;
And the stern rule it lays down for me and for you
Is to be what our friends think we are, through and through.   (37)
(Organ accompaniment "I Would be True")

A Hymn:
  (a) I Would be True, 180 ASH, 177 NHAY
  (b) It is a joy in life to find, 210 ASH. (If a is used, b could be read, or sung by a quartet.)

An Address (if desired)

The Benediction:
  O God, who art Love, grant to thy children to bear one another's burdens in perfect good will, that thy peace which passeth understanding may keep our hearts and minds in Christ Jesus our Lord.   Amen.

Services of Appreciation: Jesus

L. A SERVICE OF DEDICATION TO JESUS THE CHRIST

The Prelude

The Hymn of Praise:
  (a) When morning gilds the skies, 201 ASH, 2 NHAY *or*
  (b) Fairest Lord Jesus, 58 ASH, 137 NHAY

The Call to Worship:
>   Have you and I to-day
>   Stood silent as with Christ, apart from joy or fray
>   Of life, to see by faith His face:
>   To look, if but a moment, at its grace,
>   And grow, by such companionship, more true,
>   More nerve to lead, to dare, to do,
>   For Him at any cost?   Have we to-day
>   Found time, in thought, our hand to lay

Preparation of Services

  In His, and thus compare
  His desires with ours, and wear
  The impress of His will? Be sure
  Such contact will endure
  Throughout the day; will help us walk erect
  Through storm and flood; detect
  Within the hidden life, sin's dross, its stain;
  Revive a thought of love for Him again;
  Steady the footsteps which waver; help us see
  The footpath meant for you and me. (38)

The Choral Response (choir or congregation):
 (a) Draw thou my soul, O Christ, 370 ASH (second stanza only) *or*
 (b) O Jesus, thou art standing, 375 ASH (first stanza only)

The Scripture Reading: Mark 1: 16–20 and Lk. 9: 57–62

The Period of Silent Prayer:
 Leader: Pray that you may see Jesus Christ anew as the ideal for which your heart craves.
     (A moment of silence)
 Leader: Pray that your whole being may be made sensitive to His call to follow Him.
     (A moment of silence)
 Leader: Pray that you may be given the courage and the will to resolve deeply that you will make the venture, whatever it may cost.
     (A moment of silence)
 Leader: Pray that you may be enabled to think clearly and to understand just what your going forward with Christ will actually mean in terms of your own daily living. (39)

The Response or Hymn (if desired):
 (a) My faith looks up to thee *or*
 (b) My Jesus, as thou wilt

The Dedication (use the poem or one of the hymns):
 A.   If Christ is a man—
      And only a man—I say
     That of all mankind I cleave to Him,
     And to Him will I cleave always.

     If Jesus Christ is a god—
      And the only God—I swear
     I will follow Him through heaven and hell,
      The earth, the sea and air! (40)

 B. (a) O Jesus, I have promised, 369 ASH
   (b) True-hearted, whole-hearted, 305 HLA
   (c) Take my life and let it be, 142 ASH

The Benediction:
 The grace of the Lord Jesus Christ be with us all. Amen.
The Postlude

SOURCES

1. From *Fellowship Prayers;* slightly adapted
2. Ruth Collins
3. Bishop Scarlett
4. *Worship and Song;* adapted
5. Wade Barclay (in *Book of Worship;* adapted)
6. Harry Emerson Fosdick
7. William Adams Brown (from *The Quiet Hour*)
8. Hamlin Garland (Macmillan Co.)
9. Lee Spencer
10. J. S. Hoyland (from *A Book of Prayers*)
11. W. E. Orchard (from *The Temple*)
12. Von Ogden Vogt, *Modern Worship,* p. 68
13. From the *Churchman*
14. Herman Paul Guhse (from a *Book of Invocations*)
15. J. H. Hunter (from *Devotional Services*)
16. Phillips Brooks
17. From *The Kingdom, the Power, and the Glory*
18. A. Wakefield Slaten (from *Words of Aspiration*)
19. Author unknown
20. Robert Bartlett (from *Boy's Book of Prayers;* adapted)
21. Edna St. Vincent Millay
22. Margaret Farrend (in the *Independent*)
23. William Wordsworth
24. William L. Stidger
25. Edward Everett Hale
26. W. H. Davies
27. William Wordsworth
28. William L. Stidger
29. William L. Stidger
30. Berton Braley (in the *Delineator,* 1925)
31. Robert Bartlett
32. W. W. W. Argow
33. *Common Worship*
34. *International Journal of Religious Education*
35. William Morris
36. George Stewart (in *The Sanctuary*)
37. Edgar A. Guest (in *A Heap O'Livin'*, Reilly & Lee Co.)
38. George Klingle
39. *International Journal of Religious Education*
40. R. W. Gilder, "Song of a Heathen, 32 A.D."

CHAPTER V

WHAT MATERIALS CAN WE FIND FOR USE IN SERVICES OF WORSHIP?

Introductory: Bases of Compilation

An attempt has been made in this study to compile a large amount of material for use in worship services for college students. So far as is known, the attempt has not been made before. All the other parts of the dissertation may be considered as parts of the explanation of the selection of this material. The study has moved logically from the initial picture of dissatisfaction with existing practices to this point. Fundamental in the selection of materials is the twofold division of the purposes of college worship: ethical and appreciational. At first all the material was assembled under these two heads, being classified under many possible themes of worship. The change to an alphabetical arrangement was made after the compilation was complete, it being thought that such arrangement would be more convenient for reference purposes. The themes under which the material is now classified have undergone many changes. They were originally selected on the basis of the seven sources of worship themes outlined in Chapter IV. From those sources more than one hundred and fifty themes were secured, but, largely through a process of condensing, the number has been reduced to forty-five. The standards for planning services given in Chapter II were used throughout as criteria for the further evaluation of materials which were being considered for inclusion in the collection.

A fourth basis of selection of materials is yet to be mentioned. The college leaders of worship were asked specifically in the questionnaire to tell what materials they would like to have in a new handbook of college worship.

Question eight in the inquiry was as follows: In the light of your experience, what type of collection of materials do you think would be of the greatest benefit to you in preparing religious services for students? Sixty items were listed in forty-two replies answering this particular question. A classification of these replies follows:

1. Fourteen of the forty-two wanted a collection of prayers:

> Prayers of the present day.
> Anthology of rather *masculine, very real* prayers.
> Prayers found useful in other schools.
> Variety of prayers—such as bidding, meditative, responsive.
> Appropriate prayers for special occasions and themes.
> Wide range of responsive prayers.
> Contemporary prayers by men of acknowledged power.
> Short prayers adapted to needs of college students.
> Prayers of thanksgiving, general confession, aspiration, etc.
> Prayers adapted to the young and growing mind.
> Book of prayers.
> Might wisely print some prayers.
> Orders of service including prayers timely yet historic.
> Scripture readings with corresponding chants and prayers.

2. Twelve wanted help with regard to their hymns:

> Hymns selected with care for college students.
> A suitable hymn book.
> An adequate hymnal.
> A hymn book prepared definitely for this generation of college students.
> Hymns adapted to the young mind.
> Special hymns used in other schools.
> A collection of hymns of historic interest, with names of composers and dates. Hymns in German, French, and Spanish languages.
> Hymns, various types of ritual to provide considerable variety.
> Hymns—
> Suggestions as to hymns, etc.
> Good songs and selected responsive readings that can be supplied cheaply in large quantities.
> Might wisely print some.

3. Ten wanted responsive readings and litanies:

> Responsive readings not confined to psalms.
> Scripture responses.
> Devotional scripture; responsive readings.
> Responsive readings adapted to the young and growing mind.
> Litanies built around student needs.
> Litanies employing a modern experience.
> We could profitably use some good litanies arranged for students.
> Rich responsive readings, scriptural and otherwise. . . . I am con-

vinced of the value of all features which allow the students to take part themselves.

Responsive service true to the Christian ideals.

Good songs and selected responsive readings that can be supplied cheaply in large quantities.

4. Seven of the forty-two wanted no collection of materials:

With us the Bible is the Book of Books. Its passages are rich in poems, songs. We use others occasionally.

None, as services are now conducted.

Bible and good hymnal, to one who knows both, should be adequate. Not so much new material needed, as more worshipful leaders, men and women of spiritual discernment and faith.

I am not conscious that we need such material.

We find the strictly religious service: songs, Bible reading, short sermon, most beneficial.

Since our type of worship is not set and formal we do not feel the need of any collection of material.

No book can take the place of personal preparation on the part of the leader.

5. Six wanted complete services:

Orders of service giving complete service printed.

Various types of service.

Might wisely print some services.

Orders of service including prayers timely yet historic.

I should like to see a book containing a number of programs used in different schools.

Suggestions as to orders of worship.

6. Six wanted help with Bible selections:

A collection of Scripture readings.

Selections from God's word that are easily applied to young life.

A well-selected collection of scripture readings for college students.

A book of prayers and selections from the Bible.

Suggestions as to Bible selections, etc.

Responsive services true to the Christian ideals, including prose passages from the Bible.

7. Six wanted help with their chapel talks:

A series of brief addresses or talks on moral, religious, and educational topics presented in manner to interest students.

Book of stimulating chapel talks.

Subjects of discourses found helpful in other schools.

Inasmuch as the services are held daily, I find some difficulty in selecting themes for the talks.

Personally, I feel that a well-prepared, devotional talk, touching the life, experience, and problems of the students is the most effective.

Apt, everyday illustrations which will touch the great throbbing heart of the student whose horizon is ever widening in a collegiate atmosphere.

8. Four wanted poems:

Poems, especially great prayers.
Poetry selections.
Short poems with a vital thought for college students.
Might wisely print some.

9. Four wanted some chants:

Choir responses.
Short and concrete antiphonal material.
Might wisely print some chants.
Collection of scripture readings with corresponding chants.

10. Two wanted a worship calendar for the college year:

Themes for worship based on college seasons.
An important person or event for each school day of year.

11. One wanted modern creeds:

Short creeds which express the vital beliefs of students of to-day.

12. One wanted lists of music:

Lists of great instrumental and vocal selections.

13. One wanted "an anthology of religious and philosophical literature."

14. Seven had rather general needs:

A combination of ritual and free service.
Devotional and inspirational material.
Collections with reverent worship, action, virility, vision, and idealism.
Grouping of appropriate materials under right themes.
What is helpful seems to vary from locality to locality, and from generation to generation.
Can't say yet. My experience is too short. Am inclined to think that a general knowledge of good literature would be the best source.
Something dealing with the lives and accomplishments of great men and women who were religious; hold up their struggles, convictions, visions, determination, and behaviour in strategic moments. Let

intellectuality be the basis, make little use of sentimental or emotional efforts. Show creative thinking.

These requests from college presidents, deans, chaplains, and similar college officers, were considered very seriously in the compilation of materials. While the materials are given here primarily to facilitate the use of principles worked out in the study, it is obvious that if the materials represent too great a divergence from the practices of the colleges or ignore the purposes and wishes of those who may desire to use these helps, the study, from a practical standpoint, may not have a very extended application. Consequently, in so far as it has been found practicable to do so, the expressed preferences of actual college leaders of worship have been followed in the compilation of materials.

Nearly a third of the requests were for appropriate prayers. A large portion of the following materials are prayers, and the bibliography contains references to other collections. Considering the fact that the next most frequent request was for appropriate hymns, it is regretted that the scope of this collection could not include much along this line. Had any considerable number of colleges been using the same hymnals, more references could have been given. In the present collection reference to hymns in the *American Student Hymnal* (Century Co.) is supplied for most of the themes. This hymnal is chosen because of its special appropriateness for college use and its wide use. A number of responsive litanies, etc., are given, but the request for printed Scriptural responsive readings was not heeded for lack of space. Bible references, however, are given for most of the themes in the collection, and many of them may be used responsively. Difficulty in finding Bible readings for desired themes, as evidenced in several requests, is not uncommon. Readings which are considered usable are referred to. The request for complete services of worship is answered by the twelve illustrative services given in the preceding chapter. Printing of chapel talks was considered inadvisable, though there were several requests for such material. The themes for services given in this study may suggest topics for chapel talks. Very frequently the person who conducts the service does not give the address, and too frequently is unable to plan his service in harmony with the address. Many appropriate and readable poems are given here. A section of modern creeds is given for those leaders who believe that affirmations of faith are useful in worship. Both the worship calendars asked for have been prepared. They appear in Chapter IV.

Though this collection has been prepared mainly for the leader of college worship—the president, dean, chaplain, faculty member, student pastor, Y. M. C. A. or Y. W. C. A. workers, and any others who labor in this field, there are others who may find it useful. Pastors of churches and church school superintendents, principals, and teachers may glean assistance here. Many public school teachers in various parts of the country who conduct "opening exercises" in junior and senior high schools may find a suggestion of something different here. Persons interested in the work of the Christian Endeavor, the Epworth League, the B. Y. P. U., and similar organizations may be benefited by the use of this book. Wherever short periods of devotion are used to open meetings, leaders may find material here. The collection, however, is not a substitute for personal interest and devotion. If people do not find in these materials an expression of their own religious outpourings, they should be content to leave the book and seek elsewhere for it. Not beneath the forms of worship should the spirit of worship be found but through those forms.

Classified Index of Worship Materials

Materials for use in college worship are indexed below under the following topics:

1. Art and music
2. Beatitudes
3. Beginning of school
4. Chastity
5. Christmas
6. Church
7. Commencement; close of school
8. Consecration
9. Courage
10. Creeds
11. Deceit
12. Doubts
13. Easter
14. Education
15. Envy
16. Evening
17. Faith
18. Finances
19. Forgiveness
20. Freedom
21. Friendship
22. Health
23. Holy Week
24. Home; parents
25. Jesus, call of
26. Joy of life
27. Kingdom of God
28. Laborers
29. Martyrdom
30. Memorial
31. Morning
32. Nature
33. New Year
34. Patriotic
35. Peace (inner)
36. Peace (national)
37. Quest for God

38. Racial brotherhood
39. Repentance
40. Self-control
41. Service; love
42. Sportsmanship
43. Sunday
44. Thanksgiving; praise
45. Work

Titles of selections are followed by the last name of the authors and, where the book is listed in the bibliography which follows this section, the NUMBER of the book in that list is given. In the lists of hymns ASH refers to the *American Student Hymnal*, NHAY to the *New Hymnal for American Youth*, and HLA to the *Hymns for the Living Age*.

1. ART AND MUSIC

A. Scripture: Psalms 150; Phil. 4: 4–9
B. Hymns: 183 ASH
C. Materials:
    Prayer—Bartlett 3, p. 50; p. 52
    Prayer—Rauschenbusch 10, p. 71
    Prayer—Hartshorne, *Manual for Training in Worship*, p. 104
    Prayer—Hallock 6, p. 89
    Prayer—Douglas, *Music and Religion*
    Prayer—ASH, p. 438
    Litany—NHAY, p. 348
    Prayer—Stidger 13, pp. 62, 3
    Reading—*Girl's Every Day Book* 38, p. 55
    Reading—Hubbard 40, p. 52; p. 69
    Reading—*Good Cheer Book* 22, pp. 66–67; p. 138; p. 188

2. BEATITUDES

A. Scripture: Psalms 1; Mt. 5: 3–12; Lk. 6: 20–26; Acts 20: 32–35; I Peter 3: 8–12
B. Materials:
    Reading—Gilbran 34, p. 37
    Some Blessed—Oxenham in Hill 23, p. 640
    A Group of Sayings (responsive)—Slack 27, pp. 77–79
    Meditation—Brown 43, p. 17
    Service on—*Worship and Song* 58, p. 17

3. BEGINNING OF SCHOOL

A. Scripture: Psalms 25; Gen. 27: 41–45; Gen. 28: 10–22; Lk. 2: 41–51
B. Materials:
    Call to worship—Slaten 11, p. 11
    Prayer—Charles W. Wendt *Voice and Heart*, p. 110
    Prayer—Bartlett 3, p. 64
    Prayer—Rauschenbusch 10, p. 146; p. 35
    Prayer—Hoyland 7, p. 12

Prayer—Burton, *Fellowship Prayers*, p. 94
Prayer—Slattery 12, p. 11; p. 13
Prayer—Stidger 13, p. 47
Poem—*Silver Linings* 26, p. 84
Reading—*Social Worship* 31, p. 87
Meditation—Brown 43, pp. 71–73

4. CHASTITY

A. Scripture: Psalms 24; Pro. 7; Romans 6: 12–23; Romans 7:15–25
B. Hymns: 135 ASH, 140 ASH, 141 ASH
C. Materials:

Prayer—Rauschenbusch 10, p. 115; p. 94
Prayer—Hoyland 7, p. 107
Prayer—NHAY 54, p. 309
Reading—Gilbran, *The Prophet*, p. 57
Reading—Hill 23, p. 608
Reading—Hubbard 40, p. 94; p. 110
Reading—*Girl's Every Day Book* 38, p. 195; p. 188
Reading—Coit 30, pp. 113–19; pp. 191 ff.
Reading—Crane 32, p. 69; p. 248

5. CHRISTMAS

A. Scripture: Psalms 24, 97, 98, 8, 89: 1–36; Isa. 60: 1–5; Lk. 1: 46–55; Lk. 2: 29 ff.; Lk. 2: 4–20; Gal. 4: 1–7
B. Hymns: ASH—88, 220, 244, 245, 250, 267, 298, 302, 328, 330, 344, 360, 361; NHAY—84, 88, 101
C. Materials:

Prayer—Hallock 6, pp. 109, 110, 111
Invocations—Guhse 5, pp. 90, 91, 92, 93
Prayers—Slaten 11, p. 49; p. 53
Prayer—Porter 9, p. 126
Prayer—NHAY 54, p. 314
Prayer—Vogt, *Modern Worship*, p. 68
Prayer—Slattery 12, p. 63
Prayer—Hartshorne, *Manual for Training in Worship*, p. 59
Prayer—Bartlett 3, p. 67
Litany—Vogt, *Modern Worship*, p. 92
Litany—*The Kingdom, the Power, and the Glory* 15, p. 17
Poem—Phillips Brooks in *One Hundred and One Famous Poems*, p. 14
Poem—*Cry for Justice* 37, p. 695
Poem—*Anthology of Jesus* 24, p. 348
Poem—*Quotable Poems* 19, p. 24
Poem—*New Patriotism* 20, p. 40
Reading—*Girl's Every Day Book* 38, p. 28
Prayer after Christmas—*Girl's Every Day Book* 38, p. 405

6. CHURCH

A. Scripture: Psalms 133; Lk. 4: 16–19; Lk. 9: 49–56; John 10: 1–16; John 17: 20–26; I Cor. 12; Eph. 4: 1–16
B. Hymns: ASH: 148, 172, 224, 263, 268, 347, 381
C. Materials:
    Prayer—*Daily Devotions* 46, p. 75
    Prayer—Rauschenbusch 10, p. 134
    Prayer—*The Kingdom, the Power, and the Glory* 15, p. 74
    Prayer—Hoyland 7, p. 57
    Prayer—*Hymns for the Living Age* 55, p. 69
    Prayer—*Common Prayer* 45, p. 38
    Prayer—Brown 43, p. 111
    Litany—Stewart 50, p. 60
    Poem—*Quotable Poems* 19, p. 138
    Poem—*Poems of Justice* 18, p. 265
    Reading—Crane 32, pp. 273–77; pp. 331–37
    Litany—*The Kingdom, the Power, and the Glory* 15, p. 30

7. COMMENCEMENT; CLOSE OF SCHOOL

    Prayer—Brown 43, p. 41; p. 122
    Prayer—*Daily Devotions* 46, p. 24
    Prayer—Hartshorne, *Manual for Training*, p. 124
    Prayer—Slaten 11, p. 12
    Prayer—Hallock 6, p. 83
    Prayer—Slattery 12, p. 34
    Prayer—Bartlett 3, p. 61
    Prayer—Hoyland 7, p. 96
    Litany—*Book of Services for Group Worship* 42, p. 62

8. CONSECRATION

A. Scripture: Ex. 20: 1–17; Isa. 6: 1–9; Mt. 7: 24–27; Mt. 14: 32–36; Mk. 12: 28–34; Lk. 10: 38–42; John 6: 30–63; John 14: 21–24a; Romans 12; John 4: 31–34; I Cor. 11: 23–26
B. Hymns: ASH—74, 108, 136, 141, 142, 166
C. Materials:
    Prayer—Hoyland, *Divine Companionship* 8, p. 49
    Prayer—Hoyland 7, p. 59
    Prayer—Slattery 12, p. 15
    Prayer—Guhse 5, p. 32
    Prayer—Bartlett 3, p. 9
    Litany—*Devotional Offices for General Use*, Suter, p. 59
    Reading—*Girl's Every Day Book* 38, p. 412
    Poem—*Gradatim*, Holland
    Prayer—Guhse 5, p. 35
    Communion Prayers—Vogt, *Modern Worship*, pp. 99 ff.
    Poem—*Poems of Justice* 18, p. 153

Litany—*The Kingdom, the Power, and the Glory* 15, p. 14
Reading—Coit 30, p. 52

9. COURAGE

A. Scripture: Psalms 27; Josh. 1: 5b–7b; Mk. 2: 23–28; Mk. 3: 1–13; Lk. 12: 1–4; Acts 23: 10–27; Acts 27
B. Hymns: ASH—33, 37, 38, 83, 188, 320
C. Materials:

Prayer—*Book of Prayers* 1, p. 5; p. 9; p. 60; p. 30
Prayer—Hoyland 7, p. 111; p. 119
Prayer—Bartlett 3, p. 12
Prayer—Rauschenbusch 10, p. 144
Prayer—Slattery 12, p. 20
Prayer—*Girl's Every Day Book* 38, p. 86
Prayer—*Good Cheer Book* 22, p. 219
Reading—*Dann School Hymnal*, p. 194
Poem—*Poems of Justice* 18, p. 151
Poem—*Rhymes of a Red Cross Man*—Service, "Carry on"
Poem—*Services for the Open* 48, p. 83
Poem—Hill 23, p. 344; p. 586
Poem—*Hymnal for Young People* 57, p. 315
Poem—*Silver Linings* 26, p. 93
Poem—Wons 39, p. 64; p. 15

10. CREEDS

Guhse 5, p. 46
Rauschenbusch 10, p. 148
John Ruskin, *Fors Clavigera*, Vol. V, Letter 58
Vogt, *Modern Worship*, p. 94; p. 96
Slaten 11, p. 45
Herbert, *Good Cheer Book* 22, p. 110; p. 91
NHAY 54, p. 316
ASH 53, p. 442
HLA 55, p. 61
Hubbard 40, p. 104
Good Cheer Book 22, p. 86
Hill 23, p. 636; p. 75
Worship and Hymns, Christian Board of Publication, p. 45; p. 69
Slack 27, p. 228

11. DECEIT

A. Scripture: Amos 5: 21–25; Mt. 6: 2–6, 16–18; Mt. 23: 23–28; Lk. 11: 39–44
B. Materials:

Prayer—Hoyland 7, p. 68
Prayer—NHAY 54, p. 327
Reading—*Girl's Every Day Book* 38, p. 124

Reading—Shakespeare, "Polonius' Advice to His Son"
Poem—*Quotable Poems* 19, p. 91
Poem—*Poems of Justice* 18, p. 116
Prayer—Bartlett 3, p. 2
Reading—Coit 30, p. 79; pp. 262–64; pp. 143 ff.

12. DOUBTS

Prayer—Brown 43, p. 67
Prayer—*Book of Prayers* 1, p. 7
Poem—Hill 23, p. 216; p. 42; p. 202
Poem—*Quotable Poems* 19, p. 60
Poem—*Poems of Justice* 18, p. 69
Poem—NHAY 54, p. 327
Poem—*One Hundred and One Famous Poems*, p. 104
Poem—*Beacon Hymnal*, p. 110
Reading—Hubbard 40, p. 208
Reading—Crane 32, pp. 319 ff.
Reading—Coit 30, pp. 267–82; p. 300 (1–7)

13. EASTER

A. Scripture: Psalms 118; Lk. 24: 13–15; John 20: 1–18; I Cor. 15: 12–19, 35–44, 50–57
B. Hymns: ASH—301, 331, 333, 348; NHAY—136, 126
C. Materials:

Prayer—Guhse 5, p. 30
Prayer—Slattery 12, p. 59
Prayer—*Voice and Heart*, C. W. Wendt, p. 77
Prayer—Hallock 6, p. 74; p. 69
Prayer—Vogt, *Modern Worship*, p. 68
Reading—Garvie, *The Christian Doctrine of the Godhead*, p. 90
Poem—NHAY 54, p. 330
Poem—*New Patriotism* 20, p. 47

14. EDUCATION

A. Scripture: I Kings 3: 5–15; Pro. 3: 13–26; Pro. 4: 5–18; Pro. 8; Job 28: 7–28; Mt. 18: 1–6; Mt. 19: 13–15; Mk. 4: 1–9; John 13: 1–5, 12–15
B. Hymns: ASH—193, 299, 340, 150, 154
C. Materials:

Prayer—*Service Book of the Columbus School for Girls*, p. ii
Prayer—ASH 53, p. 441
Prayer—See various prayers in *Prayers of the Church Service League*
Prayer—Porter 9, p. 112
Prayers—*Hymnal of Praise* (Eaton) in ritual section
Prayer—HLA 55, p. 68
Prayer—Rauschenbusch 10, p. 69; p. 88
Reading—Hubbard 40, p. 21; p. 17

Prayer—Hallock 6, p. 98; p. 96
Litany—*Book of Prayers for Students*
Poem—*Worship and Hymns* (Bethany Press), p. 28; p. 98
Litany—*The Kingdom, the Power, and the Glory* 15, p. 21
Reading—Coit 30, pp. 283 ff.; p. 289 (3–13)

15. ENVY

A. Scripture: Gen. 4: 2b–12; Pro. 26: 20–26; Psalms 15; Mt. 7: 1–5; Mt. 12: 34–37; John 8: 3–11; James 3: 2–18; Mt. 6: 1–6; Mt. 23: 1–12; Mk. 10: 35–45; Lk. 14: 7–11; Lk. 18: 9–14; John 13: 1–5, 12–15; Phil. 2: 1–12; Mt. 7: 1–5
B. Materials:

Prayer—*The Kingdom, the Power, and the Glory* 15, p. 69
Prayer—*Manual of Prayers* (Catholic), p. 297
Reading—*Girl's Every Day Book* 38, p. 218
Poem—Wons 39, p. 23; p. 60

16. EVENING

A. Hymns: ASH—90, 91, 94, 96, 97, 107, 306
B. Materials:

Prayer—Rauschenbusch 10, p. 32
Prayer—NHAY 54, p. 310
Prayer—*Services for the Open* 48, p. 17
Prayer—*Worship and Song* 58, p. 93; p. 96
Prayer—*Book of Prayers* 1, p. 14
Prayer—*Daily Devotions* 46, p. 88
Poem—"The Day is Done," Longfellow
Poem—Stidger 13, p. 71; p. 30

17. FAITH

A. Scripture: Psalms 16, 23, 27, 40, 46, 62, 91, 121; Isa. 40: 27–31; Lk. 11: 5–13; Lk. 12: 22–32; Heb. 11–12: 2
B. Hymns: ASH—20, 33, 35, 37, 38, 39, 103, 152, 351, 365, 366
C. Materials:

Prayer—Hoyland 7, p. 20
Prayer—Guhse 5, p. 44
Prayer—*The Kingdom, the Power, and the Glory* 15, p. 67
Reading—*Girl's Every Day Book* 38, p. 17
Reading—NHAY 54, p. 332

18. FINANCES

A. Scripture: Deut. 8: 7–20; Deut. 15: 7–11; Ex. 32: 1–21, 30–31; Psalms 12, 41, 49; Mt. 6: 19–21; Mk. 10: 17–30; Mk. 12: 41–44; Lk. 12: 13–34; Lk. 16; I Tim. 6: 6–12; Jas. 1: 6–12
B. Hymns: ASH—60, 211, 221, 235, 86, 215, 236

C. Materials:
>   Prayer—Rauschenbusch 10, p. 65; p. 62; p. 113
>   Prayer—Hallock 6, p. 96
>   Prayer—Vogt, *Modern Worship*, p. 86
>   Prayer—Beaver 44, p. 12
>   Poem—Wordsworth, "Sonnet Written in London, Sept., 1802"
>   Poem—*Silver Linings* 26, p. 14
>   Reading—Coit 31, p. 124
>   Poem—*Cry for Justice* 37, p. 199
>   Poem—Hill 23, p. 441
>   Poems—*Poems of Justice* 18, pp. 11, 13, 40, 46, 81, 99, 100, 47, 137, 138, 145

19. FORGIVENESS

A. Scripture: Mt. 5: 38–43; Mt. 5: 44–48; Mt. 18: 21–35; Lk. 6: 30–36; Mk. 11: 25; John 8: 1–11; Romans 12
B. Materials:
>   Prayer—Rauschenbusch 10, p. 30; p. 34
>   Prayer—Goodwin 47, p. 12; p. 14
>   Prayer—*Worship and Song* 58, p. 94
>   Reading—Hubbard 40, p. 76
>   Poem—*Silver Linings* 26, p. 115; p. 38
>   Reading—Coit 30, p. 258; p. 209

20. FREEDOM

A. Hymns: ASH—110, 112, 115, 116, 121, 124, 241, 280
B. Materials:
>   Prayer—Hoyland 7, p. 64, p. 65
>   Prayer—*Worship and Song* 58, p. 95
>   Prayer—Slaten 11, p. 33; p. 52
>   Reading—*Services for the Open* 48, p. 11
>   Reading—Hubbard 40, p. 92
>   Reading—*Great Companions* 35, p. 601
>   Reading—*Poems of Justice* 18, p. 270; p. 271; p. 56
>   Poem—*New Patriotism* 20, p. 68

21. FRIENDSHIP

A. Scripture: I Sam. 20; Ruth 1; Ecc. 6: 5–17; John 15: 9–17
B. Materials:
>   Prayer—NHAY 54, p. 311
>   Prayer—Rauschenbusch 10, pp. 30 and 36
>   Prayer—*Services for the Open* 48, p. 5; p. 108
>   Prayer—Bartlett 3, p. 42
>   Litany—*Fellowship Prayers* 4, p. 64
>   Litany—Beaver 44, p. 21

Reading—Wons 39, p. 50
Poem—*A Heap O'Livin'* by Edgar Guest, p. 162
Poem—*Silver Linings* 26, p. 228; p. 10
Reading—*Girl's Every Day Book* 38, p. 116
Reading—Coit 30, p. 18; p. 206

22. HEALTH

Prayer—Bartlett 3, p. 7
Prayer—ASH 53, p. 436
Prayers—NHAY 54, p. 308; p. 324
Poem—*Good Cheer Book* 22, 115

23. HOLY WEEK

A. Scripture:

Palm Sunday: Mt. 21: 1–11
Monday: Mt. 21: 18–19; 12–17
Tuesday: Mk. 11: 20–28; Mt. 22: 34–40; Mt. 23: 1–12; John 12: 30–36
Wednesday: No record. Could use Mt. 25: 31–46; Mt. 26: 1–5; 14–16
Thursday: Mk. 14: 12–17; John 13: 1, 16, 33
Good Friday: Psalms 22, 69; Mt. 26: 26–36; Mk. 14: 43–52; Mk. 14: 53–65; Mk. 14: 66–72; John 10: 7, 9–11, 14–18; John 12: 20–33.
Saturday: Mt. 27: 62–66
Easter Sunday: See *Easter*

B. Hymns: (a) Palm Sunday; ASH—246, 349; (b) Good Friday; ASH—105, 376, 377.
C. Materials:

Prayer—Guhse 5, p. 21; pp. 26, 27, 28
Prayer—Hallock 6, p. 62; p. 60
Poem—*Poems of Justice* 18, p. 112; p. 180; p. 172
Prayer—Hoyland 7, p. 20
Prayer—Hoyland 8, p. 47 (*Divine Companionship*)
Prayer—Goodwin 47, p. 4; p. 49
Poem—*Quotable Poems* 19, p. 72
Poem—Slack 27, p. 153
Litany—*The Kingdom, the Power, and the Glory* 15, p. 25
Meditation—Brown 43, p. 37

24. HOME; PARENTS

Prayer—Hoyland 7, pp. 108, 110, 112
Prayer—Rauschenbusch 10, p. 92
Prayer—NHAY 54, p. 314
Prayer—*Services for the Open* 48, p. 21
Prayer—Bartlett 3, pp. 34, 35
Reading—Stidger 13, p. 78; p. 97

Poem—ASH 53, p. 434
Reading—Hubbard 40, p. 31
Reading—*Great Companions* 35, p. 364; p. 450
Prayer—Stewart 50, p. 55

25. JESUS, CALL OF
(See *Christmas, Easter, Holy Week*, etc.)

Prayer-Period—*Worship and Hymns* (Bethany Press), p. 28
Reading—Marchant 24, p. 252
Poem—NHAY 54, p. 460

26. JOY OF LIFE

A. Hymns: ASH—49, 51, 191, 194, 195, 196, 198, 199, 104, 205
B. Materials:

Prayer—Hoyland 7, p. 70
Prayer—ASH 53, p. 430
Call to Worship—*Worship and Song* 58, p. 93
Reading—Hubbard 40, p. 47
Reading—*Good Cheer Book* 22, p. 19
Poem—*Poems of Justice* 18, p. 228
Poem—Slack 27, p. 87
Litany—*Acts of Devotion* 2, p. 20
Reading—Coit 30, pp. 167, 237-244, 33

27. KINGDOM OF GOD

A. Hymns: ASH—61, 62, 63, 65, 155, 177, 89, 237, 249, 254, 289
B. Materials:

Prayer—Guhse 5, p. 42
Prayer—Rauschenbusch 10, p. 119; p. 121
Prayer—Hoyland 8 (*Divine Companionship*), p. 44
Prayer—*Book of Prayers* 1, p. 5
Prayer—*Daily Devotions* 46, pp. 43 and 59
Litany—Vogt, *Modern Worship*, p. 91
Reading—*The Kingdom, the Power, and the Glory* 15, p. 29; pp. 11, 13, 20
Poems—*Poems of Justice* 18, pp. 186, 201, 242, 265, 136, 138
Responsive Reading—Vogt, *Modern Worship*, pp. 12, 72, 81

28. LABORERS

Prayers—Rauschenbusch 10, p. 58; p. 53; p. 51; p. 32b
Prayer—Bartlett 3, p. 41
Prayer—Beaver 44, p. 27
Prayer—Hallock 6, pp. 90, 95
Reading—*Girl's Every Day Book* 38, p. 246
Poems—*Poems of Justice* 18, pp. 22, 143, 164, 168, 94, 237, 165, 103, 16, 92, 93

Poems—Masefield, "A Consecration"; Markham, "A Man with the Hoe"; Hood, "The Song of the Shirt"; Lowell, "A Parable."

29. MARTYRDOM

A. Scripture: See *Good Friday*
B. Hymns: ASH—113, 117, 118, 126, 146
C. Materials:

Prayer—Hoyland 7, p. 51; p. 54
Prayer—Rauschenbusch 10, p. 128
Prayer—*Book of Prayers* 1, p. 29
Poem—*Poems of Justice* 18, p. 239
Poem—NHAY 54, p. 333
Poem—Hubbard 40, p. 43

30. MEMORIAL

A. Hymns: ASH—109, 110, 112, 113, 114, 121, 128, 129, 334, 335, 336, 345
B. Materials:

Prayer—Brown 43, p. 113; p. 95
Prayer—Hoyland 7, p. 46; pp. 23, 29
Prayer—*The Kingdom, the Power, and the Glory* 15, p. 67
Poem Prayer—*Quotable Poems* 19, p. 259
Reading—Slaten 11, p. 48
Poem—*Worship and Hymns* (Bethany Press), p. 58
Poem—NHAY 54, No. 510
Reading—Coit 30, pp. 216 ff.

31. MORNING

Prayer—*Daily Devotions* 46, p. 6
Prayer—Hoyland 7, p. 113
Prayers—Rauschenbusch 10, pp. 27–31, 90
Prayer—ASH 53, p. 428
Prayer—Guhse 5, p. 88
Prayer—*Hymnal of Praise* (Eaton), by R. L. S.
Poems—*Services for the Open* 48, pp. 1, 12, 36
Poem—NHAY 54, p. 316
Poem—"To-day," Carlyle
Poem—*Silver Linings* 26, p. 113

32. NATURE

A. Scripture: Psalms 29, 93, 97, 104, 139, 148; Gen. 1; Job 38, 39; Lk. 1: 68 ff.; John 4: 19–24; Acts 17: 22–30
B. Hymns: ASH—45, 50, 51, 55, 56, 59, 161, 197, 205, 57
C. Materials:

Prayers—Hoyland 7, pp. 53, 58, 82, 17
Prayers—Rauschenbusch 10, p. 48

Prayers—Guhse 5, p. 62; p. 80; p. 64
Prayers—Vogt, *Modern Worship*, p. 73
Prayer—*Services for the Open* 48, pp. 49, 28, 32
Reading—Stidger 13, pp. 73-77, 67 ff., 60, 56, 24, 26, 19
Poem—*Good Cheer Book* 22, p. 55; p. 41
Poem—Hill 28, p. 223; p. 211; p. 32; p. 251
Poem—Hubbard 40, pp. 21, 25
Readings—*Services for the Open* 48, pp. 65, 54, 57, 61, 50, 73, xxi, 45, 29, 46, 4, 77
Poem—"The Rainy Day," Longfellow
Poem—"Flower in the Crannied Wall," Tennyson
Poem—"Leisure," W. H. Davies
Poem—"The Rhodora," Emerson
Prayer—Bartlett 3, p. 46; p. 48
Poem—"A Forest Hymn," Bryant
Prayer—NHAY 54, p. 356
Prayer—Hoyland 8 (*Divine Companionship*), p. 70
Poem—"God's World," Millay
Prayer—Brown 43, p. 76
Reading—Slaten 11, p. 17
Poem—*Poems of Justice* 18, p. 182

33. NEW YEAR

A. Hymns: ASH—30, 163, 164, 324, 339; HLA—105, 106
B. Materials:

Prayer—Hoyland 7, p. 11
Prayer—Hoyland 8 (*Divine Companionship*), p. 9
Prayer—Slack 27, p. 189
Prayer—Guhse 5, p. 11; p. 94
Prayer—Slaten 11, p. 30; p. 16
Responsive Prayer—*Worship and Hymns* (Bethany Press), p. 34
Prayer—*Good Cheer Book* 22, p. 71
Reading—Hubbard 40, p. 73
Reading—NHAY 54, p. 338
Poem—"Another Year," Katherine Lee Bates (*America the Beautiful and Other Poems*)
Poems—*Quotable Poems* 19, pp. 208, 213
Poem—*New Patriotism* 20, p. 13
Poem—*Poems of Justice* 18, p. 264

34. PATRIOTIC

A. Hymns: ASH—275, 278, 279, 281, 282, 283, 284, 286, 287, 290, 291
B. Materials:

Prayer—Hoyland 7, p. 73
Prayer—Beaver 44, p. 57
Prayer—Hallock 6, p. 118; p. 82; p. 54
Prayers—*Book of Prayers* 1, No. 67, No. 71, No. 72, No. 73

Responsive Service—*Training Young People in Worship*, Shaver and Stock, p. 215
Prayer—Porter 9, p. 136
Prayer—Guhse 5, p. 52
Reading—NHAY 54, p. 335
Aspiration—Slaten 11, p. 47; pp. 23, 20, 40, 37
Poem—*New Patriotism* 20, p. 110; pp. xiv, vi, 98, 59, 74, 85, 92
Reading—Hubbard 40, p. 178
Poem—*Quotable Poems* 19, p. 204
Reading—*Services for the Open* 48, pp. 7, 8, 10, 12
Poems—*Poems of Justice* 18, pp. 206, 215, 217, 226, 231, 244, 220, 221

35. PEACE (INNER)

Prayer—*Daily Devotions* 46, p. 91
Prayer—*The Kingdom, the Power, and the Glory* 15, pp. 68, 73
Poem—*Good Cheer Book* 22, pp. 21, 22, 23
Essay—"An Apology for Idlers," R. L. S.
Prayer—Guhse 5, pp. 41, 47
Reading—Crane 32, p. 161

36. PEACE (NATIONAL)

Prayer—Rauschenbusch 10, p. 109
Prayer—Hoyland 7, p. 121
Prayer—*Worship and Hymns* (Bethany Press), pp. 24, 25
Prayer—Vogt, *Modern Worship*, p. 86
Peace Pact—NHAY 54, p. 368
Reading—Hubbard 40, p. 33
Poem—*New Patriotism* 20, pp. 27, 36, 41, 53, 25, 6, 103

37. QUEST FOR GOD

A. Hymns: ASH—3, 5, 7, 8, 9, 10, 12, 14, 108
B. Materials:
   Prayer—Guhse 5, p. 81
   Prayer—Brown 43, p. 122
   Poem—Hill 23, p. 22
   Poem—Slack 27, p. 70
   Poem—"How the Great Guest Came," Markham
   Poem—"Christ the Man," W. H. Davies
   Prayer—Hoyland 7, p. 88

38. RACIAL BROTHERHOOD

A. Scripture: Mt. 8: 5–13; Lk. 10: 29–37; John 4: 6–24; Acts 10: 9–15, 34–43
B. Hymns: ASH—252, 255, 256, 259, 261, 270, 271, 273, 276
C. Materials:
   Prayer—*Worship and Song* (Bethany Press), p. 72; p. 95
   Prayer—*Daily Devotions* 46, p. 10

Prayer—*The Kingdom, the Power, and the Glory* 15, p. 78
Litany—*Fellowship Prayers* 4, p. 89
Poem—Slack 27, p. 200
Poem—*Poems of Justice* 18, pp. 19, 156, 157, 158, 27, 118
Prayer—Rauschenbusch 10, p. 59
Prayer—Bartlett 3, p. 38
Reading—Coit 30, pp. 201 ff.

39. REPENTANCE

A. Scripture: II Sam. 12: 1–12; Psalms 40, 51, 130, 139, 143; Ezek. 18: 19–24; Jer. 7: 1–11; Mic. 6: 6–8; Isa. 55: 6–9; Lk. 7: 36–50; Lk. 15
B. Hymns: ASH—42, 76, 212, 214, 217, 223, 226, 227, 229, 230, 231, 258, 383
C. Materials:

Prayer—Rauschenbusch 10, p. 126
Prayer—*Daily Devotions* 46, p. 12
Aspiration—Slaten 11, p. 29
Prayer—Goodwin 47, p. 23
Prayer—Coit 31, p. 21
Prayer—Vogt, *Modern Worship*, p. 77
Prayer Poem—*Quotable Poems* 19, p. 189
Litany—Porter 9, pp. 157 ff.
Litany—*Services for the Open* 48, p. 16
Litany—*Training Young People in Worship*, Shaver and Stock
Reading—Vogt, *Modern Worship*, p. 79
Poem—*Poems of Justice* 18, p. 42
Prayer—Hoyland 7, pp. 114, 120
Reading—Coit 30, p. 52

40. SELF-CONTROL

A. Scripture: 1. Self-control—Pro. 20: 1; Pro. 23: 29–35; Isa. 5: 11–23; Mt. 23: 23–28; Mk. 3: 1–6; John 2: 13–17; Eph. 4: 24–32. 2. Temptation—Psalms 119: 33–40; Mk. 7: 14–23; Mk. 8: 31–37; Lk. 4: 1–13; Lk. 6: 43–48; Eph. 6: 10–18; Romans 7: 14–25; Jas. 1: 12–27
B. Materials:

Prayer—ASH 53, p. 431; p. 432
Prayer—Rauschenbusch 10, p. 111
Prayer—Goodwin 47, p. 24
Prayer—Slattery 12, p. 43; p. 49
Prayer—Brown 43, p. 140
Prayer—Hill 23, p. 447
Reading—Drummond, *Greatest Thing in the World*, pp. 23 ff.
Poem—Browning, "Temptation"
Reading—*Great Companions* 35, p. 273
Reading—Coit 30, pp. 64, 107–112, 37, 203 ff., 82

41. SERVICE; LOVE

A. Scripture: Lev. 19: 9–18; Pro. 3: 3, 4; Isa. 53; Isa. 61; Micah 6: 6–8; Mt. 5: 23, 24; Mt. 25: 31–46; Mk. 10: 42–45; Lk. 10: 25–37; I Cor. 13
B. Materials:

> Prayer—Hoyland 7, p. 13
> Prayer—Goodwin 47, p. 13
> Prayer—Stidger 13, p. 43
> Prayer—*Daily Devotions* 46; p. 7; p. 27; p. 4; p. 63
> Aspiration—Slaten 11, p. 43
> Reading—*Book of Services* 42, p. 51
> Guided Prayer—Coit 31, p. 84
> Poem—Hunt, "Abou Ben Adhem"
> Poem—*New Patriotism* 20, pp. 115, 76
> Poem—*Worship and Hymns* (Bethany Press), p. 291
> Poem—*Silver Linings* 26, p. 78
> Poem—*Poems of Justice* 18, p. 176; pp. 199, 242, 248, 243
> Reading—Crane 32, pp. 155–157
> Service—Stewart 50, p. 63

42. SPORTSMANSHIP

A. Hymns: ASH—158, 159, 169, 179
B. Materials:

> Prayer—*Services for the Open* 48, p. 85
> Prayer—*Services of Worship for Boys*, Gibson, p. 85
> Prayer—Bartlett 3, p. 6
> Prayer Poem—Berton Braley, *The Delineator*, 1925
> Poem—"The Conquered" in *Poems of Action*, D. R. Porter

43. SUNDAY

A. Scripture: Mk. 1: 21–35; Mk. 2: 23–28; Lk. 6: 1–10; Lk. 13: 10–17; John 5: 5, 8–10; John 9: 13–16
B. Materials:

> Prayer—Slattery 12, p. 55
> Responsive Prayer—*Hymnal for Young People* 57, p. 281
> Reading—Stidger 13, p. 89
> Prayer—Rauschenbusch 10, pp. 37, 38

44. THANKSGIVING; PRAISE

A. Scripture: Psalms 8, 65, 46, 92, 96, 100, 103, 136, 146, 147, 148, 149, 150; Lk. 17: 11–19; Col. 1: 9–19
B. Hymns: ASH—46, 157, 199, 197, 204, 239, 303, 338, 18, 21, 23, 25, 26, 27, 40, 49, 59, 354, 357, 387, 389
C. Materials:

> Prayer—Hoyland 7, p. 62; p. 82
> Prayers—Bartlett 3, pp. 66, 67

Prayer—Stidger 13, p. 21
Prayer—Hallock 6, p. 106; p. 103
Prayers—*The Kingdom, the Power, and the Glory* 15, pp. 70, 71, 1, 50 ff.
Litany—Coit 31, pp. 89 ff.
Litany—*Acts of Devotion* 2, p. 2
Litany—NHAY 57, p. 291; p. 23
Litany—*Beacon Hymnal*, p. 26
Prayer—ASH 53, p. 437 (also pp. 425–427)
Reading—Hubbard 40, p. 78
Reading—*Great Companions* 35, p. 565
Poem—NHAY 57, p. 320; p. 312
Poem—*Quotable Poems* 19, p. 53
Poem—*Silver Linings* 26, p. 185
Poem Prayer—*Worship and Hymns* (Bethany Press), p. 27

45. WORK

A. Scripture: Pro. 6: 6–11; Pro. 24: 20–24; Lk. 13: 6–9; I Thess. 4: 11–12; II Thess. 3: 10–12
B. Materials:

Prayer—Hoyland 7, p. 36; p. 96
Prayer—Rauschenbusch 10, p. 102
Prayer—Goodwin 47, p. 52
Litany—*Book of Prayers for Students*, Part IV
Reading—Hubbard 40, p. 59
Reading—Marchant 24, pp. 160 ff.
Poem—*Services for the Open* 48, p. 20
Poem—Wons 39, p. 57
Poem—*Worship and Hymns* (Bethany Press), p. 91; p. 92; p. 29
Poem—"To-morrow" by Edgar Guest in *A Heap O'Livin'*

BIBLIOGRAPHY OF MATERIALS FOR USE IN COLLEGE CHAPELS

* Indicates first rank in usefulness
† Indicates useful but not essential

I. Collections of Prayers

1. *A Book of Prayers.* Commission on Evangelism and Devotional Life of the Federal Council of the Federal Churches of Christ in America. Pp. 32. 5¢. A splendid collection of eighty prayers from a variety of sources. Worth much more than the price would indicate.

2. *Acts of Devotion.* S. P. C. K., A. R. Mowbray and Co., London. A little booklet of responsive services approved by the Church of England for use after the office. Conservative enough to satisfy the orthodox; yet distinctly modern in its outlook.

3. Bartlett, Robert Merrill. *A Boy's Book of Prayers.* Pilgrim Press, 1930. Pp. 71. 50¢. A new companion volume to the *Girl's Book*.

The book promises to be popular. Most of the prayers, however, are in first person, and they seem to be intended for use with boys of high school age.

4. *Fellowship Prayers.* Woman's Press, revised 1928. Pp. 126. $1.00. An anthology of prayers prepared for the Y. W. C. A. Covers their needs very well.

†5. Guhse, Herman Paul. *A Book of Invocations for Use Throughout the Year.* Fleming H. Revell, 1928. Pp. 94. $1.00. Short, usable prayers for various times in the year: the Christian holy days, at the sea shore, autumn, etc.

6. Hallock, G. B. F. *Cyclopedia of Pastoral Methods.* George H. Doran Co. Pp. 270. Prayers, dedicatory forms, and ceremonies. For the pastor, not the college chaplain, though there are many prayers appropriate for chapel use.

*7. Hoyland, J. S. *A Book of Prayers Written for Use in an Indian College.* Challenge Books and Pictures, Ltd., London, 1921. Pp. 122. 80¢. Beautiful prayers of universal appeal dealing with thanks, humility, freedom, love, purity, hope, death, etc.

8. Hoyland, J. S. *The Sacrament of Common Life, The Four-Fold Sacrament, The Sacrament of Nature, The Divine Companionship, God in the Commonplace.* Volumes of excellent original prayers of great spiritual insight. Written in the style of *Prayers for Use in an Indian College,* but these volumes are smaller and contain fewer prayers for college use. *God in the Commonplace* may be useful.

9. Porter, David R. *The Enrichment of Prayer.* Association Press, 1918. $1.25. A rather conventional collection of prayers gathered from devotional literature from Biblical times to the present.

*10. Rauschenbusch, Walter. *Prayers of the Social Awakening.* Pilgrim Press, 1909. Pp. 154. $1.00. Among the most helpful prayers ever written for this generation. Prayers of a real social passion. Prayers from this book are included in nearly every modern collection of prayers.

†11. Slaten, Arthur Wakefield. *Words of Aspiration.* Privately printed, 1927. $1.50. Used in the West Side Unitarian Church of New York in place of the invocation. These forty-nine "words" may be useful as calls to worship or may be adapted to prayer use.

12. Slattery, Margaret. *A Girl's Book of Prayers.* Pilgrim Press, 1914. Pp. 60. 50¢. A much used little volume. Prayers were written chiefly for college students.

13. Stidger, William L. *Pulpit Prayers and Paragraphs.* George H. Doran Co., 1926. Pp. 208. $1.75. Prayers of free style and "beatitudes of the beautiful" in nature which many will like. His "Pulpit Editorials" are interesting and may suggest chapel talks.

14. Suter, John W. *Devotional Offices for General Use.* Century Co., 1928. Brief services in the Anglican style, compiled mainly from

offices used in the Cathedral Church of St. Paul, Boston, and from *A New Prayer Book*.

†15. *The Kingdom, the Power, and the Glory.* Oxford University Press, 1925. Pp. 84. 50¢. Part III of a notable English experiment in modern prayer book making. Contains some excellent litanies and prayers.

16. Tileston, Mary Wilder. *Prayers Ancient and Modern.* Little, Brown and Co., $1.50. A revised edition of a well-known collection. Contains many usable prayers, but the percentage of them which would appeal to college students appears not to be large.

II. Collections of Poetry

17. Ault, Norman, compiler. *The Poet's Life of Christ.* Humphrey Milford, London, 1922. Pp. 275. Somewhat like Marchant's *Anthology*. Poems follow the life of Jesus chronologically. This collection has a splendid historical perspective in showing what English-speaking people have said about Jesus, but as it purposely avoids an emphasis on the later poets its value for college chapel is lessened.

*18. Clark, Thomas C. *Poems of Justice.* Willett, Clark, and Colby, 1929. Pp. 306. $2.50. Poems, mostly modern, of social and industrial justice.

*19. Clark, Thomas C. and Gillespie, Esther A., compilers. *Quotable Poems.* Willett, Clark, and Colby, 1928. Pp. 374. $2.50. A book which is valuable to leaders of college worship because the poems are "quotable" and combine a "modern tone" with "deep spiritual qualities." 500 inspirational poems of 300 poets.

†20. Clark, Thomas C. and Gillespie, Esther A., compilers. *The New Patriotism.* Bobbs-Merrill Co., 1927. Pp. 127. Poems of the "new patriotism" based, as Edwin Markham says in the Foreword, "on the Fraternity of the Peoples, based on social justice and world brotherhood."

†21. Harrington and Thomas, compilers. *Our Holidays in Poetry.* H. H. Wilson Co., 1929. Pp. 480. A collection of poems for use on Lincoln's birthday, Easter, Arbor Day, Mother's Day, Thanksgiving, and Christmas. The book gains in value by having been limited in scope of subject matter, and gains in "readability" by having been planned primarily for children.

22. Herbert, Blanche E. *The Good Cheer Book.* Lothrop, Lee, and Shepherd Co. Pp. 344. $1.50. Poems and prose passages from varied sources with the general theme of cheerfulness.

*23. Hill, Caroline Miles. *The World's Great Religious Poetry.* Macmillan Co., 1926. Pp. 836. $2.00. Deservedly one of the most popular collections of religious verse. It contains poems of all nations and all times. Thoroughly indexed.

24. Marchant, Sir James, editor. *Anthology of Jesus.* Harper and Brothers, 1926. Pp. 419. An anthology of the life and work of Jesus

composed of prose and poetry of the traditional type, selected almost entirely from writers of the past.

25. Schauffler, Robert Haven. *The Poetry Cure.* Dodd, Mead and Co. $2.50. An interesting anthology of poems of cheer and courage.
26. *Silver Linings.* George Sully and Co., 1927. Pp. 247. $1.50. Popular poems of inspiration and courage.
27. Slack, Elvira. *Christ in the Poetry of Today.* Woman's Press, 1928. Pp. 287. A delightful volume of modern American poetry dealing with Christ. Periods in his life, and his influence, are well covered in poems representing modern thought.
28. Stewart, George. *Redemption: An Anthology of the Cross.* George H. Doran Co., 1927. A collection of poems of all times dealing with the Cross. It appears that all viewpoints have been represented in this versatile work. Not a great number, however, lend themselves readily to oral reading in chapels.

III. Collections of Chapel Readings

29. Cluett, Robert. *Responsive Scriptures.* Association Press, 1922. 50¢. Sixty-two responsive readings from the Bible for church or home. Of doubtful value for general use in colleges.
*30. Coit, Stanton, compiler. *The Message of Man.* Macmillan Co., 1894. Pp. 340. "A book of ethical scriptures gathered from many sources" to make an astonishingly valuable book for chapel readings.
31. Coit, Stanton and Scott, Charles Kennedy. *Social Worship.* West London Ethical Society, 1913. A "Bible" of English Humanism in the first volume, and a hymnal and chant book in the second. Introductory sentences, meditations, lessons, chants, hymns gleaned and adapted from countless sources. A stupendous work, but perhaps less valuable to the average leader of American college worship than Dr. Coit's earlier work, *The Message of Man.*
32. Crane, Dr. Frank. *Why I am a Christian.* William H. Wise and Co., 1924. A book of the short articles which made Dr. Crane so famous. These deal with religious perplexities. Their viewpoints may be helpful to many college students. They are quite readable.
33. Fosdick, Harry Emerson. *The Manhood of the Master.* Association Press, 1913. Pp. 175. Comments on Bible readings dealing with qualities in the character of Jesus.
34. Gibran, Kahlil. *Jesus the Son of Man.* Knopf, 1928. Pp. 216. A collection of short sketches purporting to be the accounts of various incidents in the life of Jesus as told by his contemporaries, probably half of them Bible characters, half fictitious. Some of the sketches are beautifully conceived and make acceptable chapel readings.
*35. Leavens, Robert French. *Great Companions.* The Beacon Press, 1927. Pp. 678. $3.00. A priceless book for leaders of worship who desire collections of extra-Biblical material for the "reading." This

anthology of inspirational passages was gathered from a wide variety of ancient and modern sources. One may find something on almost any theme, a statement which is true also of *The Message of Man*. The main difference is that the latter treats topics in chapters consisting of carefully woven short quotations from different writers, while in *Great Companions* each selection is by a single author, but the selections are grouped according to topics.

36. Merrifield, Fred. *Modern Religious Verse and Prose*. Charles Scribner's Sons, 1925. Pp. 471. A splendid anthology of modern (partly contemporary) religious literature. The compiler was not searching for passages for oral reading; hence a great many of the selections are a little too difficult for that purpose.

†37. Sinclair, Upton. *The Cry for Justice*. The John C. Winston Co., 1915; Upton Sinclair, 1921. Pp. 891. An attempt "to cover the whole field of the literature of social protest, both in prose and poetry, and from all languages and times." The result is praiseworthy. We are given numerous examples of "radical" literature concerning: toil, outcasts, revolution, mammon, Jesus, the church, war, patriotism, Socialism, etc.

38. *The Girl's Every Day Book*. Woman's Press, 1926. Pp. 435. $1.25. A book of excellent readings on topics which concern every thoughtful girl.

39. Wons, Anthony. *Tony's Scrap Book*. Reilly & Lee Co., 1930. Pp. 88. $1.00. A book of poetry and prose which proved to be popular in "Tony's" radio programs of homely moralizing.

40. Hubbard, Elbert. *Elbert Hubbard's Scrap Book*. Roycrofters, 1923. Pp. 228. Just what the title indicates. Among this mass of material one may find gems of prose and poetry for chapel use.

41. Holmes, John Haynes, and others. *Readings from Great Authors*. Dodd, Mead and Co. $1.00. A brief collection of readings prepared for use in the Community Church, New York. The range of topics is limited, and the readings, while "great," are not all suited to public or responsive reading.

IV. Books of Services of Worship

42. *A Book of Services for Group Worship*. Woman's Press, 1929. Pp. 63. $1.00. A Y. W. C. A. collection of seventeen services prepared by various people. Some of them are suitable for general college chapel, while others are useful only for Y. W. C. A. meetings.

†43. Brown, William Adams. *The Quiet Hour*. Association Press, 1926. Pp. 148. $1.50. Brief services of meditation used at Union Theological Seminary. Meditations are planned to include prayers on verses of Scripture and periods of silence. There are thirty services.

44. Beaver, Gilbert A. *New Ventures of Faith*. Interchurch World Movement, 1919. Pp. 72. 15¢. Suggestions for thirty-one services of worship. Has some good forward-looking materials.

45. *Common Prayer.* The book of the services and ceremonies of the Protestant Episcopal Church. Has exerted a tremendous influence on general Protestant worship.
46. *Daily Devotions.* Commission on Evangelism and Devotional Life of the Federal Council. Pp. 95. 15¢. Scripture, poem, prayer on selected topics for three months' use. Some topics may be suggestive for further development.
47. Goodwin, Frank J. *The Vigil at the Cross.* Macmillan Co., 1925. Pp. 75. Material for Good Friday services, grouped about the seven words. Prayers and devotional literature.
†48. Mattoon, Laura L. and Bragdon, Helen D. *Services for the Open.* Century Co., 1924. Pp. 212. $1.00. Services of worship based on nature themes, e.g., "For a rainy day, Birds of the Air, the vesper hour." Includes a section of hymns. A commendable collection of material from which much may be secured even if the services are not used as printed.
49. Morrell, Belle and Huber, Laura. *Christmas Preparatory Services.* Woman's Press, 1924. Pp. 18. 30¢. Three services of worship for Christmas, one honoring Jesus, one an inter-racial service, and one a service of the Christmas story. Useful.
50. Stewart, George. *The Sanctuary.* Association Press, 1928. Pp. 118. 50¢. Twenty-five well-planned and unified services on modern worship themes: beauty of the world, peace, labor, friendship, etc.
51. *The Fellowship of Prayer.* Committee on Evangelism and Devotional Life of the Federal Council. Pp. about 30. 2¢. Brief meditations and prayers for individual devotions during Lent. A new edition is published each year. Useful for Lenten chapel services.
52. Hazeltine, Mary Imogene. *Anniversaries and Holidays.* American Library Association, 1928. Pp. 228. A convenient and complete calendar of happenings for each day in the year, with bibliographies. The leader of worship who wishes to utilize birthdays and historical anniversaries as well as the common religious holy days should find this book of great assistance.

V. School Hymnals

*53. *American Student Hymnal*, edited by H. Augustine Smith. Easily the most outstanding hymnal of our day prepared mainly for college use. The abundance of new hymns expressive of modern emphases in religion occasionally confuses the new user at first, but there is little in the book which is not up to college standards in intelligence, dignity, and vigor. Published in 1928, it is already in use in about 70 colleges and universities. The hymnal contains 385 hymns, 20 chants and responses, and 83 pages of readings and other worship helps. Century Co., $1.35 in quantities of fifty or more.

*54. *The New Hymnal for American Youth*, edited by H. Augustine Smith. Published late in 1930, this hymnal has already been adopted by several educational institutions. This book possesses the same high standards of the preceding hymnal, but it was planned for students just a little younger. Those who feel that the "American Student Hymnal" contains material too difficult for present use will be delighted with this second hymnal which, on the whole, is somewhat simpler and may be more practical for many undergraduate institutions. It contains 344 hymns and 85 pages of worship material. Century Co., 85¢ in quantities of fifty or more.

55. *Hymns for the Living Age*, edited by H. Augustine Smith. A few colleges, desiring a hymnal with a modern viewpoint and with high musical standards, adopted this hymnal which was published in 1926—before either of the school hymnals mentioned above. The hymnal was intended primarily for church use, and is excellent for that purpose. Century Co., $1.35 in quantities.

56. *The Association Hymnal*, Woman's Press, 1922. This hymnal of the Y. W. C. A. is used in a few women's schools. It contains 135 hymns, most of them old and well known. There are several responses of merit.

57. *The Hymnal for Young People*, edited by Milton S. Littlefield and Margaret Slattery. An excellent and thoroughly usable hymnal for young people. Plenty of the universally known hymns, but those not adapted to the religious expression of adolescents have been omitted. Chronological index of hymns. Several oratorio selections and responses. Nineteen brief services of worship. A. S. Barnes and Company, New York, 1928.

58. *Worship and Song*, edited by Benjamin S. Winchester and Grace Wilbur Conant. Pilgrim Press, 1921. Planned primarily for use in church schools of religious education, and best suited for that purpose, this hymnal nevertheless has many features to commend it to junior colleges and other undergraduate institutions who desire a hymnal which has quality without being too difficult. Contains a number of services of worship planned for young people by Frank M. Sheldon.

59. *The Methodist Hymnal*, Methodist Book Concern, 1905. The hymnal in use in the chapels of most Methodist schools. This hymnal has most of the faults to be expected in a hymnal which has gone so long without revision. It contains most of the old stand-bys, but few of the hymns of the social gospel and only those hymns for youth which may be culled from the hymnody of the past.

60. *Inter-Church Hymnal*, compiled by Frank A. Morgan, published by Biglow and Main, 1930. $1.00 in quantities. Hymns were selected on the basis of modern Protestant usage. Results are much better than one would expect. President Palmer of Chicago Theological Seminary compiled the section of worship materials, which is perhaps the most complete to be found in any hymnal. Hymns are poorly classified.

APPENDIX

A. THE QUESTIONNAIRE

A BRIEF INQUIRY

For Aid in Conducting College Chapel

Name of school: Location:

Name of person reporting: His position:

1. A. Does your school conduct regular (1) chapel or (2) assembly services in which there is a religious or devotional element? If so, check 1 or 2 as the case may be.
   B. On what days and during what hours is it held?
2. A. If the worship service is a part of a longer assembly, state about how much time is usually given to the worship.
   B. Does the school have a chaplain or a corresponding officer? Underscore the answer: Yes   No
   C. What other position in the school (if any) does he hold?
   D. If there is no chaplain, who has charge of the worship services?
3. A. Is there usually an address as a part of the worship service? Underscore the answer: Yes   No
   B. Of what length?   C. By whom?
4. A. What hymnal or song book do you use?
   B. If it does not fully meet your needs, please state why.
5. Check which you use in your worship service:
   A. Quartet ....: male   female   mixed
   B. Chorus or choir ....: male   female   mixed
   C. Single soloist or song leader ....
   D. No musical leadership except from chaplain or chairman ....
6. List some things which have been done to provide what you consider a suitable atmosphere for the devotional service.
7. Will you be willing to share your experiences with others by listing the books of prayers, poems, songs, chants, services, or plays which have been of most help to you in planning your devotional services?
8. In the light of your experience, what type of collection of materials do you think would be of the greatest benefit to you in preparing religious services for students? Please be specific: your answer will help in the preparation of such a book.
9. A. What do you hope to accomplish with your worship services? (Your fundamental purposes of worship are desired. Try to avoid vague, general statements.)

B. What evidence of success have you?
10. A. What materials might you include in a worship service for students based on the theory you gave in 9A?
11. A. What percentage of your students and faculty attend chapel?
   B. To what extent is attendance required?
12. A. How would you describe in a few words the prevailing student attitude toward chapel in your institution?
   B. To what extent do you estimate that there is student sentiment for radical change either in the conduct of worship or in attendance rules?

A REQUEST.—Sample worship programs from your school may be helpful in this study, and will be appreciated. Please send them with this inquiry, if convenient to do so.

B. LIST OF COÖPERATING SCHOOLS

One hundred seventy-six questionnaires were sent out as follows:

   78 to private colleges and universities
   38 to publicly controlled colleges and universities
   25 to junior colleges
   13 to normal schools
   12 to teachers colleges
   10 to theological seminaries

The following schools returned questionnaires:

Allegheny College
Amherst College
Antioch College
Asbury College
Ashville Normal School
Baylor University
Bethel College
Beloit College
Bethany College (Kansas)
Biblical Seminary in New York
Boston University School of Theology
Brigham Young University
Centre College
Clark University
Colby College
College of Idaho
College of the City of Ashville
College of William and Mary
College of Wooster
Cornell University
Dartmouth College
Defiance College
Denison University
Drake University
Drew Theological Seminary
Drury College
Duke University School of Religion
Earlham College
Elon College
Emory University
Garrett Biblical Institute
Gettysburg College
Goucher College
Harvard University
Hebron College
Henderson State Teachers College
Hendrix-Henderson College
Hiram College
Indiana State Teachers College
Intermountain Union College
Junior College, Alderson, W. Va.
Junior College, Highland Park, Mich.
Junior College, Phoenix, Ariz.
Kent State College
Knox College
Lehigh University
Lincoln University (Mo.)
Mary Baldwin College
Michigan State Normal College
Morton Junior College (Ill.)
Mount Union College
Oberlin College
Occidental College
Oklahoma A. and M. College
Oklahoma Presbyterian College for Girls
Otterbein College
Ozark Wesleyan College
Parsons College
Rollins College
Rutgers University
St. Olaf College
Shenandoah College
Smith College
State College for Teachers (Albany, N. Y.)
State Normal School, Fairmont, W. Va.
State Normal School, Frostburg, Md.
State Normal School, Gorham, Me.

State Normal School, New Haven, Conn.
State Normal School, Plattsburg, N. Y.
State Teachers College, Fresno, Cal.
State Teachers College, Harrisonburg, Va.
State Teachers College, Slippery Rock, Pa.
State University of Nevada
Storer College
Southern Baptist Theological Seminary
Susquehanna University
Texas Christian College
Texas Christian University
The Mason School
Tulane University
University of Alabama
University of California
University of Colorado
University of Delaware
University of Illinois
University of Michigan
University of North Carolina
University of Oregon
University of South Dakota
University of Redlands
University of Rochester
University of Vermont
University of Virginia
University of Wisconsin
University of Wyoming
Vassar College
Wabash College
Walla Walla College
Ward-Belmont School
Washington and Lee University
Waynesburg College
Western Theological Seminary
Wilberforce University
Williams College
Winthrop College
Yale University

C. BOOKS LISTED IN REPLIES TO QUESTIONNAIRES AS HAVING BEEN OF VALUE IN THE PREPARATION OF SERVICES FOR COLLEGE WORSHIP

(Listed according to frequency of mention)

World's Great Religious Poetry—Hill
Prayers of the Social Awakening—Rauschenbusch
The Meaning of Prayer—Fosdick
The Sanctuary—Stewart
Book of Common Prayer
Chapel Service Book—Stevens and others
Bible Readings—Thomas and Espenshade
  (One reply each for the following)
Great Companions—Leavens
Quotable Poems—Clark
Prayers Written for Use in an Indian College—Hoyland
Services for the Open—Mattoon and Bragdon
Illustrated Bible Readings—Craft
Bible Selections—Buell and Wells
Bible Readings—Schaeffer
Presbyterian Book of Common Worship
Book of Services for Group Worship—Woman's Press
Poems of Justice—Clark
Social Worship—Coit
Services and prayers for church and home—Thirkield
The Temple—Orchard
Prayers of the Massachusetts Church Service League—Pilgrim Press
Enrichment of Prayer—Porter
"Toc H" Manual
Everyday Prayers—British Student Movement
Daily Meditations
God's Minute
Half Way to Noon—Dovey
Art of Life—Ellis
Treasury of the Humble—Maeterlinck
Preface to Morals—Lippman
Hymns for the Living Age—Smith
Parish School Hymnal—United Lutheran
Hymnal of Praise—Eaton
Unitarian Hymnal
Various modern translations of the Bible

D. BIBLIOGRAPHY

AMES, E. S. *Religion.* Henry Holt & Co., New York, 1929.
ANGELL, ROBERT COOLEY. *The Campus.* D. Appleton Co., New York, 1928.
BENNETT, CHARLES A. "Worship and Theism." *The Journal of Religion*, November 1926, pp. 570–85.
BENNETT, CHARLES A. "Worship in Its Philosophical Meaning." *The Journal of Religion*, September 1926, pp. 486–503.
Biennial Survey of Education 1926–1928. Department of the Interior, Bureau of Education. U. S. Government Printing Office, Washington, D. C., 1930.
BOYER, EDWARD STERLING. "Religious Education in Colleges, Universities, and Schools of Religion." *Christian Education*, October 1927, pp. 2–6.
BOYER, EDWARD STERLING. *Religion in the American College.* Abingdon Press, New York, 1930.
BROWN, INA C. "Kagawa Diagnoses American Religion." *The Christian Century*, September 24, 1930, p. 1147.
BROWN, WILLIAM ADAMS. *Worship.* Association Press, New York, 1917.
BYINGTON, EDWIN H. *The Quest for Experience in Worship.* Doubleday, Doran & Co., Garden City, N. Y., 1929.
CABOT, R. C. *What Men Live By.* Houghton Mifflin Co., Boston, 1914.
CHARTERS, JESSIE BLOUNT. *The College Student Thinking It Through.* Abingdon Press, New York, 1930.
Christian Education, February 1930. Number Devoted to Survey of American College Chapels.
COE, GEORGE ALBERT. *A Social Theory of Religious Education.* Charles Scribner's Sons, New York, 1917.
COE, GEORGE ALBERT. *The Motives of Men.* Charles Scribner's Sons, New York, 1928.
COE, GEORGE ALBERT. *What Ails Our Youth?* Charles Scribner's Sons, New York, 1924.
COIT, STANTON, Editor. *Social Worship.* West London Ethical Society, London, 1913.
COLE, STEWART G. "What Is Religious Experience?" *The Journal of Religion*, September 1926, pp. 472–85.
COMFORT, W. W. "The Friends' Theory of Worship." *The Christian Century*, March 19, 1930, pp. 336, 367.
CONKLIN, EDMUND S. *Psychology of Religious Adjustment.* Macmillan Co., New York, 1929.
GAVIT, JOHN PALMER. *College.* Harcourt, Brace and Co., New York, 1925.
GIBSON, H. W. *Services of Worship for Boys.* Association Press, New York, 1914.

HARPER, EARL ENYEART. *Church Music and Worship.* Abingdon Press, New York, 1924.

HARRIS, CYRIL. *The Religion of Undergraduates.* Charles Scribner's Sons, New York, 1926.

HARTSHORNE, HUGH. "Rethinking the Function of Worship." *Religious Education*, December 1928, pp. 967-73.

HAWKES, HERBERT E. *College—What's the Use?* Doubleday, Doran & Co., Garden City, N. Y., 1927.

HENKE, F. G. *A Study in the Psychology of Ritualism.* University of Chicago Press, Chicago, 1910.

HEPHER, CYRIL, Editor. *The Fellowship of Silence.* Macmillan Co., New York, 1917.

HITES, LAIRD T. *The Effective Christian College.* Macmillan Co., New York, 1929.

HOCKING, WILLIAM ERNEST. *The Meaning of God in Human Experience.* Yale University Press, New Haven, Conn., 1912.

HODGKIN, L. VIOLET. *Silent Worship.* Swarthmore Press, London, 1919.

HOLMES, JOHN HAYNES. "A Humanistic Interpretation of Prayer." *The Christian Century*, October 16, 1929, p. 1276.

HUNTER, STANLEY A. *Music and Religion.* Abingdon Press, New York, 1930.

JONES, RUFUS. *New Studies in Mystical Religion.* Macmillan Co., New York, 1927.

KEPHART, A. P. "The Problem of College Chapel Exercises." *Educational Review*, March 1926, pp. 146-52.

LAMPE, M. WILLARD. "The World Students Live In." *Christian Education*, March 1929, pp. 352-61.

LEONARD, EVENDEN, AND O'REAR. *Survey of Higher Education for the United Lutheran Church in America.* Bureau of Publications, Teachers College, Columbia University, New York, 1929.

LINDBLOM, ROSS C. "College as It Might Be"; in *The Students Speak Out!* New Republic, Inc., New York, 1929.

LITTLE, CLARENCE C. *The Awakening College.* W. W. Norton & Co., New York, 1930.

MACINTOSH, DOUGLAS C. "What is Worship?" *Religious Education*, December 1930, p. 946.

OTTO, RUDOLF. *The Idea of the Holy.* Revised Edition. Oxford University Press (American Branch), New York, 1925.

PRATT, JAMES BISSETT. *The Religious Consciousness.* Macmillan Co., New York, 1920.

Religion in the Colleges. Princeton, 1928. Galen M. Fisher, Editor. Association Press, New York, 1928.

Religious Education, October 1925, p. 362. Anonymous Communication from a College Junior.

ROSS, G. A. J. *Christian Worship and Its Future.* Abingdon Press, New York, 1927.

SCLATER, J. R. P. *Public Worship of God.* George H. Doran Co., New York, 1927.

SHAVER, ERWIN L. AND STOCK, HARRY THOMAS. *Training Young People in Worship.* Pilgrim Press, Boston, 1929.

SIMPSON, ROBERT S. *Ideas of Corporate Worship.* T. & T. Clark, Edinburgh, 1927.

SOARES, THEODORE GERALD. *A Dictionary of Religion and Ethics.* Macmillan Co., New York, 1921.

SOARES, THEODORE GERALD. "The Meaning of Worship." *International Journal of Religious Education,* November 1929, pp. 9, 10.

SMITH, ROBERT SENECA. *If Worship Meant Something to Me.* Association Press, New York, 1930.

SPERRY, WILLARD. *Reality in Worship.* Macmillan Co., New York, 1926.

STEWART, G. WAUCHOPE. *Music and Church Worship.* Hodder and Stoughton, London, 1926.

STOCK, HARRY THOMAS. "Church Work with Students." *Christian Education,* April 1930, p. 431.

STREETER, B. H., Editor. *Concerning Prayer.* Macmillan & Company, Limited, London, 1916.

STREETER, B. H., Editor. *The Spirit.* Macmillan Co., New York, 1919.

STRICKLAND, F. L. *Psychology of Religious Experience.* Abingdon Press, New York, 1924.

SWISHER, WALTER SAMUEL. *Music in Worship.* Oliver Ditson Co., Boston, 1929.

TUFTS, JAMES HAYDEN. "A University Chapel." *The Journal of Religion,* September 1926, p. 450.

TWEEDY, HENRY W. "The Problem of the College Chapel." *Religious Education,* February 1927, pp. 136–41.

VOGT, VON OGDEN. *Modern Worship.* Yale University Press, New Haven, Conn., 1927.

WEIGLE, LUTHER ALLEN AND TWEEDY, HENRY HALLAM. *Training the Devotional Life.* Pilgrim Press, Boston, 1919.

WIEMAN, HENRY NELSON. "How Religion Cures Human Ill." *The Journal of Religion,* May 1927, p. 264.

WIEMAN, HENRY NELSON. *Methods of Private Religious Living.* Macmillan Co., New York, 1929.

WIEMAN, HENRY NELSON. *Religious Experience and Scientific Method.* Macmillan Co., New York, 1927.

WIEMAN, HENRY NELSON. *The Wrestle of Religion with Truth.* Macmillan Co., New York, 1928.